SOCIAL CHANGE AND COMMUNITY POLITICS IN URBAN JAPAN

Edited by JAMES W. WHITE and FRANK MUNGER

Contributors:

Christie W. Kiefer
G. Ralph Falconeri
Margaret A. McKean

COMPARATIVE URBAN STUDIES

MONOGRAPH NO. 4

Institute for Research in Social Science
University of North Carolina at Chapel Hill
1976

International Standard Book Number: 0-89143-047-4
Library of Congress Catalog Card Number: 77-851

Institute for Research in Social Science
University of North Carolina at Chapel Hill

Cover design by Patricia Ramay Sanford

CONTENTS

PAPERS

> Manchester: "Shock City" of the 1840s
> Chicago, London, Los Angeles as Shock Cities
> Today's "Shock City": Tokyo
> Densities, *Danchi*, and Political Attitudes
> Urbanization and Environment: Protest Mobilization
> Metropolitan Government for the Shock City
> References

> Introduction
> *Danchi* Residents
> Social Aspects
> The *Danchi* and Future Politics
> Conclusion
> References

> Perspectives
> Toward Defining Modernization
> The Case of Saiwai-cho
> Replacing the Chonaikai: Political and
>   Administrative Changes
> Conclusions
> Appendix A
> References

iii

LIST OF TABLES

LIST OF FIGURES

LIST OF ILLUSTRATIONS

I

SOCIAL CHANGE AND URBAN LIFE: AN INTRODUCTION

*Frank Munger**

"Every age has its shock city." Such is the suggestion of
the English historian Asa Briggs. Every age will have a city
notable not necessarily for its size, certainly not necessarily
for its beauty or its success, but for the fact that it appears
to epitomize the historical forces at work remaking urban life.
To this city both foreign and domestic visitors will flow in
search of understanding, for it is this "shock city" that must
be known if cities are to be known at all (Briggs, 1965).

MANCHESTER: "SHOCK CITY" OF THE 1840s

For Briggs, Manchester was the "shock city" of the world
of the 1840s. In sheer numbers it was not remarkable; although
Manchester had grown from 40,000 to 142,000 between the 1780s
and the 1830s, it could not rival London--already over the million
mark in the 1820s--in size. What was remarkable was the new economic order being created: the first, clearly defined, urban
end-product of the Industrial Revolution.

To some the vista was horrifying. General Napier, sent to
command troops there during a period of labor violence, described
Manchester in 1838 as "the chimney of the world. Rich rascals,
poor rogues, drunken ragamuffins and prostitutes...(T)he only
view is a long chimney: what a place! The entrance to hell realized!" The *Manchester Guardian* was more enthusiastic about
what it saw within its own community and claimed uniqueness:
"The manufacturing system as it exists in Great Britain, and the
inconceivably rapid increase of immense towns under it, are without previous parallel in the history of the world."

The *Guardian* might be accused of local exaggeration, but
others saw the city as equally remarkable. Thomas Carlyle, after

---

*Frank Munger is Director of the Institute for Research in Social Science and
Professor of Political Science at the University of North Carolina, Chapel Hill.

a visit to Manchester, found the city "every whit as wonderful,
as fearful, as unimaginable as the oldest Salem or prophetic
city." He saw it, however, as built "upon the infinite abysses,"
and Disraeli agreed. Disraeli saw "two nations" in Manchester,
a total division of classes, and warned: "How are manners to
influence men if they are divided into classes--if the population
of a country becomes a body of sections, a group of hostile gar-
risons?"

It was precisely this characteristic of social conflict,
the concomitant of the factory system, that attracted and fascinated visitors, though not all drew Disraeli's conclusions.
Frederich Engels, who claimed to know Manchester as well as his
own Rhineland, saw the same things and concluded that Manchester
was "the classic type of modern industrial town." Within it
urban life would "weld the proletariat into a compact group with
its own ways of life and thought and its own outlook on society."
In an industrial city, feudalism could end only in a successful proletarian revolution. And if Engels' prophecy has not
yet come true, Manchester's factory feudalism did at least, appropriately enough, extend itself politically to the rest of
Britain in the rival forms of Chartism and the Anti-Corn Law
League, while producing the intellectual export of the "Manchester
School" of Richard Cobden and John Bright.

CHICAGO, LONDON, LOS ANGELES AS SHOCK CITIES

If Manchester is for Briggs the "shock city" of the first
half of the nineteenth century, Chicago is its successor as the
"shock city" of the 1890s. Again the visitors flocked in; Cobden's advice to a friend departing for America was: "See two
things in the United States, if nothing else--see Niagara and
Chicago." Once more, what they saw was not entirely pleasant;
Rudyard Kipling remarked after a visit that having seen Chicago
he "urgently desired never to see it again." W.T. Stead, a
British journalist, suggested the tone of his remarks by the
title of his book, *If Christ Came to Chicago*, published in 1893.
But not all visitors from abroad were as critical. While acknowl-
edging that many of his compatriots saw Chicago as a "purposeless
hell," Henry Trueman Wood, secretary to the Royal Commission for
the British Section of the Chicago Exhibition of 1893, dissented,
calling it a "wonderful city," more interesting than any English
provincial city or even London itself.

The "White City" of Chicago on display at the World's Colum-
bian Exhibition of 1893 was indeed one demonstration of Chicago's
power and impressiveness. Another was the skyscraper. Although

New Yorkers may find it difficult to believe, the *American Slang
Dictionary* of 1891 defined a skyscraper as "a very tall building
such as now are being built in Chicago." But what repelled--or
aroused--foreign visitors most was the brawling vitality of its
population, their seemingly infinite ethnic variety, the slums
within which they lived, and the ethnic and social conflicts
they created. Carl Sandburg's "bold strong slugger among your
soft cities" was also the Chicago of Upton Sinclair's *The Jungle*
(published in 1906) and a generation later (in 1922) of Bertolt
Brecht's "Jungle of Cities." And the invitation of Brecht in
his prologue to *In the Jungle of Cities: The Fight Between Two
Men in the Gigantic City of Chicago* had already been followed
by many, similarly fascinated, foreign visitors: "You are in
Chicago in 1912. You will witness an inexplicable wrestling
match between two men and observe the downfall of a family that
has moved from the prairies to the jungle of the big city. Don't
worry your heads about the motives for the fight, keep your mind
on the stakes. Judge impartially the technique of the contenders,
and be prepared to concentrate on the finish" (Brecht, 1971).

Chicago did have one rival as a "shock city" in the 1890s,
though Briggs does not appear to classify it as such. London
at the end of the nineteenth century attracted attention by its
unbelievable bigness. The London of Sherlock Holmes was "the
largest city in the world" and to contemporaries seemingly limit-
less. Using French analogies Taine described it as 12 cities
the size of Marseilles, 10 as big as Lyons, and 2 as large as
Paris. "Words on paper are no substitute for the effect on the
eyes. You have to spend several days in succession in a cab,
driving out north, south, east and west, for a whole morning,
as far as those vague limits where houses grow scarcer and the
country has no room to begin" (Briggs, 1971).

What Manchester was to the 1840s and Chicago (or London)
to the 1890s, Los Angeles was to the 1930s and the 1940s--or so
Briggs tells us. Lewis Mumford did not see it thus. Writing
in 1938 in his classic *The Culture of Cities*, Mumford provides
8 page references to Manchester, 7 to Chicago, and 11 to London,
but only 1 to Los Angeles (Mumford, 1938). Yet in his beloved
New York City (12 references) the World's Fair of 1939 and 1940
was to place on display in its Perisphere a motor city of automobiles and expressways that Los Angeles was to realize in the
postwar period. The "shock city" was now the automobile city,
a sprawling metropolis of suburbs linked by freeways and a central
city partly abandoned, partly obliterated by vehicles with over
half its land area given over to streets, highways, and parking
lots. In this present other cities saw their future. The sub-
urbanized "Organization Man" seemed peculiarly Californian, but

was in fact to be--for Whyte at least--from Chicago (Whyte, 1957) and was soon to be recognized everywhere from Toronto (see Seeley, Sim, and Loosley, 1956) to the Levittowns (see Dobriner, 1963; Gans, 1967).

TODAY'S "SHOCK CITY": TOKYO

Manchester, Chicago, London, and Los Angeles: What do they have in common with Tokyo? It is my contention that what these cities were in the past, Tokyo is today and will be in the immediate future: the "shock city" of now and of time ahead. Tokyo has today the same horrifying fascination that London had 80 years ago, unbelievable bigness; but if Taine could measure London's size in a cab, only a helicopter would do justice to Tokyo.

Today Tokyo has replaced London in the competition for size, but the scale has changed. As Barbara Ward has pointed out, Tokyo has the "dubious distinction" that by 1985 this single urban center--or, as the English would say, conurbation--will bring together 25 million people. In 1900 there were no more than 11 cities of over a million in population--with 6 of them in Europe. By 1950 there were 75 cities of such size, 51 in developed regions, 24 in the developing world. Today there are 191 with 101 in developing nations, and by 1985 there may be 273 with 147 in developing nations (Jackson, 1976).

To these Tokyo provides a model, but it is in a more exclusive club. By 1985 there should be at least 17 cities of *ten million or more*, and of these Tokyo is expected to be the largest. The change has come abruptly; if we take Lewis Mumford's 1938 book once more as a reference mark, Tokyo finds no place in it, though Mumford finds space to mention Toledo (Ohio) and Torino. For Tokyo, increase in size has brought increase in problems. One of these is, of course, the necessity to provide an economic base for such a large urban population, and on this score Japan's achievement has been remarkable. In other respects, however, Japan's example has been less edifying. The photographs of Eugene Smith have dramatized the cost in industrial pollution and its human victims (Smith and Smith, 1975). In one of the papers that follows, Margaret McKean describes Japan as "the world's leader in pollution diseases." The tremendous problems of air pollution in the Tokyo Bay area when temperature inversions occur were dramatized in 1971 by the issuance of gas masks. American television screens have been presented with a version of Tokyo commutation--where over three quarters of the commuters travel by subway or railway--in which "pushers" pack

travelers closer together by brute force. In 1975 when New
York City appeared to be teetering on the edge of municipal
bankruptcy, so also was Tokyo.

The question is whether such magnitudes and such densities
of urban population are viable. After decades of expressed
doubt, some have insisted that density of population does not
in itself increase crime, mental illness, or other indicators
of pathology (Freedman, 1975). But can such numbers, at whatever density of concentration, be maintained? Tokyo, as Jonathan
Freedman notes, is the test case, a city of very great size and
of very high density that--he claims--actually works. And in
what is particularly important to the cities of the developing
world, works at low levels of technology in which, for example,
"honey-bucket trucks" are still used to gather night soil from
the central wards of Tokyo. The papers below, first presented in
a panel session at the Annual Meeting of the Association for Asian
Studies in San Francisco in April 1975, address themselves to
some, though not all, of the questions that arise from city size
and density. They do not deal directly with fiscal or administrative structure but, as the title indicates, with "Social
Change and Community Politics in Urban Japan." Both opinion
polls and official measures of "disutilities" agree that (1) pollution and (2) commuting are the most serious of Japan's urban
problems, and ramifications of both are treated below.

DENSITIES, *DANCHI*, AND POLITICAL ATTITUDES

The common thread that runs through these papers is their
political focus. Although one was written by an anthropologist,
one by an historian, and two by political scientists (by disci-
plinary affiliation), all agree in emphasizing the primacy of
political attitudes and behaviors in the resolution of urban
problems. The first paper, Christie W. Kiefer's "Leadership,
Sociability, and Social Change in a White-Collar *Danchi*," is
concerned primarily with the formation of political attitudes,
and focuses on one of the aspects of Japanese urban life most
easily generalizable to the experience of other nations. The
post-World War II world saw a proliferation of high-density
residential developments in western Europe, eastern Europe,
the United States, South America, Hong Kong, and elsewhere, all
aimed at pressing problems of housing shortage. The Japan Housing Corporation, patterned after Britain's public building corporations under the New Towns Act, similarly constructed large
numbers of apartments in a frantic effort to meet a very serious
shortage of residential housing. In the early seventies the
rate of housing construction in Japan was one of the highest in
the developed world, although the backlog of demand was also
large. The Japanese call these apartment complexes, typically

4 to 5 stories, with 16 to 30 very small apartments, *danchi*.
Usually built in new communities peripheral to existing urban
centers, they raise all the questions of community structure
we associate with the word suburbanization. As high-density developments in the vertical dimension they raise even more acute-
ly the question dismissed by Freedman: The viability of humane
life in crowded urban space.

Pearl Jephcott has summarized much of the literature concerning the social and human costs of high-rise construction and
added to it a study of Scotland. Some conclusions are overpower-
ing in their weight: whether in Ballymun outside Dublin or as a
substitute for Glasgow's Gorbals, high-rise residential development is "nae use for the bairns," and separates the child on the
ground from his/her home in the sky (Jephcott, 1971). The height
of the typical *danchi* is less and the social impact presumably
less severe, but as Jephcott notes the frequency of complaints
about loneliness in the midst of many, so Kiefer reports on its
equivalent, what Japanese describe as *ikuji noiroze* (child-
rearing neurosis), which results from the isolated life of women
in *danchi*. Its complement is the life of a husband and father
separated from the daytime existence of his residential community,
with no attachment of ownership or ability to make meaningful
additions or repairs to his home, and looking forward constantly
to the opportunity to "move up" to better housing.

Kiefer concludes that "*danchi* life imposes new forms of social life on residents and...these new experiences...alter political behavior," and then speculates as to the direction of the
changes involved. One effect, he argues, is increased opportunity
for political participation by females. Male *danchi* dwellers
are typically passive politically, waiting for external decisions
to be made for them--an orientation toward politics natural under
the circumstances but reinforced by a distinctive Japanese style
of personal commitment to the economic organization that provides employment. Such male passivity opens opportunities for
female political activity at the same time that the rationalization of household upkeep provides increased available time.
Kiefer sees *danchi* political activity as involving female challenges to male-dominated governmental organizations in various
realms, but particularly in respect to education.

More broadly, Kiefer suggests that *danchi* life provides an
imitative attitude set in which keeping up with the neighbors
(and maintaining agreement with them) assumes great importance.
Drawing on Dobriner's "visibility principle," he argues that
people emphasize what they know can be seen by others (Dobriner,
1963). In graphic form, where each *danchi* apartment has its

balcony for drying clothes and airing bedding, and this requires
maintaining respectability of appearance. The implications are
more substantial, however, for "visibility" in the *danchi* can
only be of material things, and Kiefer believes that the possibility of a visible status based on nonmaterial accomplishments
is lost with the demise of a community possessing personal knowledge of its inhabitants. This interpretation, he suggests, is
consistent with Young and Wilmott's studies of East London
(Young and Wilmott, 1957). If true, the conclusion is an important one, for it implies that the advocates of "personaliza-
tion" in mass architecture (Pawley, 1971) may be unaware that they
are dealing with only part of the problem and are seeking to
create an architectural world in which personality is to be expressed primarily through material. The political implications
are also important for the imitative style applies also to the
formulation of political attitudes and the development of political behaviors.

In the last of the papers, James W. White uses survey data
from Tokyo neighborhoods to explore similar questions. His data
support Kiefer's notion that *danchi* life is conducive to increased political participation by women. One motivation is provided by an educational system under very high pressure, more
intense perhaps than any other developed nation in the world including Great Britain in the worst excesses of the "eleven-plus."
Under such circumstances parentage of a school-age child strongly encourages political involvement. In general, White finds
that parents, home owners, and long-time residents are more likely
to be involved with the community.

Some of White's most interesting conclusions concern class
differences as they affect political participation in the *danchi*,
and his findings contribute to our general knowledge of the political implications of suburbanization. Clark called attention
to the fact that not all Toronto suburbs are "Crestwood Heights"
(Clark, 1966) and Berger identified the insufficiency of a model
of suburbanization that ignored the "Working-Class Suburb"
(Berger, 1960). White's conclusions are in many ways strikingly
similar to Berger's; in Japan, White finds an important distinction between blue-collar workers who see *danchi* life as an at-
tainment--and wish to make the *danchi* a community--and white-
collar workers who see the *danchi* as a way station with home
ownership as the ultimate goal. Kiefer likewise calls attention
to this aspect of white-collar *danchi* life and notes the buildup
of political frustration as the "cooling off" of the Japanese
economy appears to endanger these hopes.

URBANIZATION AND ENVIRONMENT: PROTEST MOBILIZATION

If Kiefer and White are contributing to an increasingly
extensive cross-national literature on the effects of *suburbanization* and apartment life on values, the other two papers represent contributions to a similarly extensive literature on *urbanization* and its impact. In particular, these authors address
questions such as how communities come to be mobilized to protest government actions their citizens see as threatening to
their interests, and what the consequences of such protests may
be. In an urban world where protest seems pandemic, their concerns are surely timely.

G.R. Falconeri's "Impact of Rapid Urban Change on Neighborhood Solidarity: A Case Study of a Japanese Neighborhood Association" is a case study of a neighborhood community in the
middle-sized Japanese city of Kanazawa threatened by one of the
classic problems of modern urban development: a street widening
through an older neighborhood of small shops and residences. In
this case study members of the neighborhood association--though
with some misgivings--did nothing to protest and accepted the
decision. The results could have easily been anticipated: The
neighborhood shopping center was destroyed as many shops were
torn down, and many (especially younger) housewives found it more
convenient to shop elsewhere in larger establishments now ac-
cessible via the easier transportation route provided. (Interestingly, in terms of the topic discussed above, those dispos-
sessed by the street widening were offered priority assignments
to *danchi* housing but declined.)

While Falconeri is concerned with *petite histoire* and a
kind of event familiar to urbanists elsewhere, in "Citizens'
Movements in Urban and Rural Japan," Margaret McKean seeks to
generalize the circumstances under which environmental concerns
precipitate the formation of protest organizations. One thread
running through her account is the distinction between rural and
urban protest movements. Protest, she finds, may develop either
in the "traditional" rural or in the "modern" urban setting. In
urban areas, as in the western Tokyo cases McKean cites, resistance to construction projects seen as threatening to established
values may develop in upper middle-class neighborhoods. If
Falconeri's neighborhood residents had organized to defend their
shops against encroachment, they would have constituted such a
group. But concern over pollution is often greatest, McKean
suggests, in semirural areas where new industrial complexes have
created massive pollution precisely because treatment facilities
appear unnecessary in the rural setting. In their account of
the mobilization of the Minamata community against mercury

poisoning of fishing waters--the Minamata disease--the Smiths have provided a book-length photographic essay on just such an event (Smith and Smith, 1975). In rural areas protest may at times appeal also to a basic agrarian and anti-industrialist sentiment not unlike the traditionalist agrarian values occasionally expressed by American southerners.

McKean finds that environmental complaints are more frequently articulated in urban areas. This is not necessarily, she argues, because the problems are more severe there, but may be because urban values are more conducive to the expression of protest. At this point her argument returns us to the views presented by Kiefer and White in respect to the social values developed through *danchi* living.

But McKean also identifies a structural characteristic that facilitates protest in the urban neighborhood and defines the course it will follow. The protesting urban community sees its enemies as outsiders intent on injuring the neighborhood; no one within the petty community is likely to have strong reasons to support the change. The enemies to the organizers of protest to be found in the neighborhood are only indifference and apathy--not hostility. This was certainly true in the case that Falconeri cites; although the *chōnaikai-chō* was convinced the project would be good for the neighborhood and sought to convince the residents of its value, no powerful self-interest in the Kanazawa community supported the street widening. Inaction resulted from passivity.

The case is quite different within a rural community because it is a community in quite a different sense: not an urban community of *danchi* look-alikes, but a community of complementary yet contradictory parts. If some protest pollution, others fear the loss of their jobs. The organizers of rural protest find their antagonists within their own communities, almost certainly occupying positions of established influence.

From these differences in situation, McKean traces a number of differences between the two groups of activities. Activists in rural protest movements tend to be drawn from the ranks of the traditional parties; urban activists from the left opposition. Urban protesters tend to be experienced in community action and concerned with broader issues; the rural protesters are inexperienced and narrowly focused on the problem at hand. The rural protester protests the process of urbanization; the urban protester protests the products of urbanized society.

METROPOLITAN GOVERNMENT FOR THE SHOCK CITY

To this point no particular attention has been paid to the metropolitan level of government, either as politics or as administration. The focus of all four papers is upon the attitudes and behaviors of local communities within the whole. It seems appropriate to conclude this introduction, therefore, by seeking to draw out some of the implications of the studies for metropolitan government. As I state that question, it becomes one of ideology: Is there any ideological base from which urban policies can be evaluated and those who see them in like terms brought together as political allies?

Certainly it is hard to find such a base in the traditional ideologies of left, center, and right--in Japan or elsewhere. Until the late 1960s at least, both left and right in Japan shared a common commitment to industrialization. This was, in fact, one of the major political problems facing the protest movements, as McKean calls to our attention. Right-wing politicians could be depended upon to oppose a protest movement; left-wing politicians might take it up as a device to embarrass the government but lacked any ideological commitment to it. In rural areas McKean finds some evidence that participation in protest caused some switching to the left-wing parties among previously conservative activists, pleased and surprised at the help offered by the left to their cause; in urban areas participation in protest appeared to have little effect upon national party identifications. Neither party grouping provided, however, a dependable basis of support for protest. As Falconeri notes, "(I)n Japan modernity--however defined--is welcomed."

Yet not always. Falconeri may be correct insofar as elites are concerned, but McKean documents the existence of both urban and rural protest against at least the forms in which modernity is cloaked. Any movement that might challenge the general commitment to modernity would require, however, some bridge between "traditional" and "modern," rural and urban, protests. From her contacts with protest activists, McKean sees further development along this line unlikely and does not expect to see the protest movements coalescing into any kind of national force. According to McKean, Japanese protest activists see national politics as too remote and impervious to influence to be of interest. In this she believes they are realistic.

But need they be interested in national politics? Any answer requires analysis of the sources of control over community decision-making, and American social scientists have disputed so bitterly over the question as to leave many battle fatigued and fleeing from the field of academic combat. Question and answer lie at the core of the dispute between pluralists and elitists over the proper interpretation of power structure in community and nation. Protest movements form; they win occasional victories. On just such a fact--the defeat of tin-can housing by an aroused neighborhood community--Robert Dahl constructed much of the pluralist edifice of his classic study, *Who Governs?* (1961). But are such victories frequent enough to be meaningful in defining power? Can a consumer movement win individual victories over retailers and distributors or must it do battle with national corporations through national politics? Can environmentalists fight a successful series of local battles or must they declare war on an economic system that demands environmental pollution?

One purported answer is provided by a structural alternative to the traditional economy-based ideologies of left-center-right, the ideology of decentralization. Rather as the Progressive Movement in early Twentieth Century America expected that a change in the way decisions were made would necessarily produce a change in the quality of the decisions reached, so advocates of decentralization appear to assume that a change in structure will produce a change in outcomes. One of the more intriguing findings reported in *The Changing American Voter* is the reversal within mass opinion of the ideological meaning given to the statement that government has become too big. This view, generally associated with conservative political ideology as recently as 1960, by 1972 had come to be an article of liberal faith and was expressed more frequently by those who called themselves liberals (Nie, Verba, and Petrocik, 1976). The change may not surprise us too much; it indicates the breadth of adoption of the creed "Small is beautiful." It suggests also the new ideological underpinning for the doctrine of decentralization.

Again the Japanese experience has provided us with data--and should provide us with more. After the Second World War, Tokyo municipal government was reorganized into Tokyo Municipal Government with a federal structure dividing powers between a central unit and 23 wards, plus a number of cities, towns, and villages in the suburbs and outlying areas. Like the reorganization of London into the Greater London Council described by Smallwood (1965), this reorganization took the form of a decision of the national government imposed by fiat upon the local governments in the urbanized area. There is also, of course, a rough equivalence in the structural arrangement of federalism with London's "Metropolitan Borough" corresponding to Tokyo's wards. The Japanese city's arrangement is the more complex, however, with a third tier of still smaller neighborhood units (*machi*) which are the subject of White's paper.

What conclusions in respect to decentralization and its possible meanings in other settings do these papers provide? Since they are not focused explicitly on the topic, they can do no more than suggest possibilities. White clearly believes that the neighborhood units can be meaningful communities and urges that they be given additional functions: In particular that the school districts so important to Japanese parents be made coterminous with the neighborhoods.

Falconeri's account is also relevant, even if the city is of smaller size. Noteworthy is his comment that although a Kanazawa City League of Neighborhood Associations exists, it is unwilling to intervene to use its influence when only a single neighborhood is in trouble. The most significant aspects of the case study by Falconeri concern, however, an experiment underway in that city in which paid employees of an Administrative Liaison Service System are replacing the locally elected, unpaid leaders of the neighborhood associations in many of their functions. Decentralization may be an ideology, but centralizing tendencies are still strong currents. Appropriately enough, one paid employee of the Kanazawa Liaison Service System is quoted by Falconeri as attributing "ideology" to those neighborhood associations resisting the liaison system.

Finally, McKean's paper can be used once again to develop a point made before, but often obscured in the polemics over decentralization. Just as protest means different things in rural and urban settings, decentralization of decision-making will have different consequences in different environments. In the rural or semirural, industrializing community, giving more real power to the local governmental unit means creating a microcosm of the national conflict over the value to be attached to development; for better or worse neighbors will argue, face-to-face, over what they want their community to be.

Such communities are heterogeneous. As McKean reminds us, urban "communities," if defined as neighborhoods, are not. Their enemies lie outside a homogeneous community, and that is to say that those who may suffer by the decisions--given community control--will have no voice in their making. It is this ambiguity that has always plagued the decentralization movement, and an American reader will be reminded of it by White's suggestion of a greater coherence through geographical congruence of neighborhoods and school districts. In the American context "decentralization of educational decision-making" and the "neighborhood school" seem somehow to be talking about similar things, but with directly opposed ideological values attached.

In hopelessness, some have abandoned the goal of decentralization and have accepted the inevitability of nationalized decision-making. If still actuated by the goal of change, they turn to efforts to create national structures of countervailing power. It is possible there is an alternative: to create devices for decentralized decision-making that provide intimacy of scale and personal involvement without a balkanized city composed of hostile neighborhoods governed on the principle of the Polish Diet that one negative vote paralyzes action. Hopefully, further study of urban Japan and its "shock city," Tokyo, may contribute to such understanding.

REFERENCES

Berger, Bennett M. *Working-Class Suburb: A Study of Auto Workers in Suburbia.* Berkeley: University of California Press, 1960.

Brecht, Bertolt. *Collected Plays: Volume I.* New York: Pantheon Books, 1971.

Briggs, Asa. *Victorian Cities.* Amer. Ed. New York: Harper and Row, 1965.

Clark, Samuel Delbert. *The Suburban Society.* Toronto, Canada: University of Toronto Press, 1966.

Dahl, Robert A. *Who Governs?* New Haven, Conn.: Yale University Press, 1961.

Dobriner, William M. *Class in Suburbia.* Englewood Cliffs, N.J.: Prentice Hall, 1963.

Freedman, Jonathan L. *Crowding and Behavior.* New York: Viking Press, 1975.

Gans, Herbert J. *The Levittowners: Ways of Life and Politics in a New Suburban Community.* New York: Pantheon Books, 1967.

Jackson, Barbara Ward. *The Home of Man.* New York: Norton, 1976.

Jephcott, Pearl. *Homes in High Flats.* University of Glasgow Social and Economic Studies Occasional Papers No. 13. Edinburgh: Oliver and Boyd, 1971.

Mumford, Lewis. *The Culture of Cities*. New York: Harcourt, Brace, and Co., 1938.

Nie, Norman H., Sidney Verba, and John R. Petrocik. *The Changing American Voter*. Cambridge, Mass.: Harvard University Press, 1976.

Pawley, Martin. *Architecture versus Housing*. New York and Washington: Praeger Publishers, 1971.

Seeley, John R., R. Alexander Sim, and Elizabeth W. Loosley. *Crestwood Heights: A Study of the Culture of Suburban Life*. New York: Basic Books, 1956.

Smallwood, Frank. *Greater London: The Politics and Metropolitan Reform*. Indianapolis: Bobbs-Merrill, 1965.

Smith, W. Eugene, and Aileen M. Smith. *Minamata*. New York: Holt, Rinehart, and Winston, 1975.

Whyte, William Hollingsworth. *The Organization Man*. Garden City, N.Y.: Doubleday, 1957.

Young, Michael, and Peter Wilmott. *Family and Kinship in East London*. London: Kegan-Paul, 1957.

II

LEADERSHIP, SOCIABILITY, AND SOCIAL CHANGE IN A WHITE-COLLAR DANCHI

*Christie W. Kiefer**

INTRODUCTION

The public mass apartment housing known as Kōdan Jūtaku *danchi* in Japan is politically interesting for a number of reasons. First, it is itself in part a political creation. The builder of this apartment housing, the Japan Housing Corporation (Nihon Jūtaku Kōdan), was established largely as a vote-getting measure, and it is one of the oldest and by far the largest builder of mass apartment housing in the country, with some 700,000 units and over two million residents. Second, the large Kōdan *danchi* apartment towns have an artificial effect on the politics of their surrounding areas because they both create new local governmental problems, and often differ from local norms in the political attitudes of their inhabitants. The focus of this paper, however, will be on a third intriguing facet of the Kōdan Jūtaku *danchi*--the fact that *danchi* life imposes new forms of social life on residents and that these new experiences themselves alter political behavior.

First, we will define more clearly the term Kōdan Jūtaku *danchi*, and indicate how this type of housing fits into modern urban Japan. The word *"danchi"* refers to large modern apartment complexes that are open to anyone who can afford the rent. The term includes privately and cooperatively owned apartment buildings, publicly owned buildings other than relief housing

*Christie W. Kiefer is Associate Professor of Anthropology in Residence in the Department of Psychiatry and Associate Director of the Human Development Program at the University of California, San Francisco. The research on which this article was based was supported in part by a grant from the National Institute of Mental Health.

for low-income families, and the huge housing complexes built
by the Japan Housing Corporation. It generally denotes middle-
class housing, and so carries an economic as well as an architectural message. Old-fashioned apartments, small buildings,
and company-owned housing for workers, along with large, expensive quarters for the well-to-do are excluded from the definition of *danchi*. The largest, most widespread, and best-known
type of *danchi* is that built by the Japan Housing Corporation
--the Kōdan Jutaku *danchi*. This paper is restricted to this
type in the interest of clarity and brevity, and is based
on a study by the author in 1965-66. Below is a brief description of this type of *danchi*.

In the mid-1950s the Japanese government was still strug-
gling with an urban housing crisis of disastrous proportions.
At the end of the war, one-fifth of the Japanese population
had been without housing of any kind. A program of low interest loans for new construction and makeshift housing for
the destitute had taken some of the pressure off the upper and
lower strata of Japanese society, but there remained the problem of the growing young urban white-collar class. These
people, by virtue of their educations and occupations, were a
kind of elite, and yet they could not afford adequate housing
anywhere near the major cities where they worked. The creation
of the Japan Housing Corporation in 1955 was an attempt to deal
with the problem of white-collar housing; it was patterned
after the public building corporations founded in postwar
Britain under the New Towns Act.

The Housing Corporation had two main goals. First, inexpensive mass rental housing was to be constructed for middle-
income families--that is, families whose income totaled at
least five and one half-half times the rental rates of the
housing units. In 1960 the average monthly income of the Japan
Housing Coporation tenant was slightly higher than the average
for urban wage earners, and nearly twice the nationwide average (Kasamatsu, 1963). Tenants also tended to be employed by
large industries in white-collar occupations. The men tended
to be college graduates. The largest age groups for entering *danchi* residents are 25-40 years old for men, and 20-30
for women.

The Housing Corporation's second objective was to develop
tracts of unused land near urban centers. These tracts were
to be densely settled in an effort to deflate the cost of surrounding residential land and thereby bring real estate

ownership within the means of middle-income families in the cities. This goal does not seem to have met with much success.

By 1971, sixteen years after its creation, the Japan Housing Corporation had built 639,000 dwellings on 51,900 acres of land--housing about two million people. Between 1968 and 1973, Corporation housing amounted to about 5% of the nation's total new construction. Most of these dwellings are built, either for rental or for sale, in large housing complexes on unused or redeveloped land near large metropolitan centers--that is, *danchi* in the true sense of the word. Some of these complexes house upward of 100,000 souls and the colossal Tama New Town in Tōkyō has a target population of 410,000.

Physically, the white-collar *danchi* resembles a giant apiary. It is an orderly cluster of very large buildings, usually four or five stories tall and containing from 16 to 30 identical apartments each. The apartments are tiny, even by Japanese standards. They average, for instance, about one-third the size of the apartments in Park Forest, Illinois. This tiny space, about 250 to 300 square feet, is laid out for "rational" use, like a trailer or a boat, so that there is a minimum of wasted space. Each apartment is self-sufficient, having its own tub, toilet, kitchen, living room or rooms, and a balcony for drying clothes and airing bedding. With the exception of *tatami* (straw mat) flooring and sliding paper interior doors, materials are durable and require little maintenance. The small size and "rationalized" layout of the *danchi* apartments reduces housekeeping tasks to a minimum, and, with the help of their electrical and gas appliances, women can run the home with a fraction of the time and effort necessary even in present-day "traditional" types of housing. There are no collective facilities within the buildings where people live--no laundry rooms, storage rooms, lobbies, or game rooms. Community activities are concentrated in centralized service areas where the resident finds shops, schools, meeting halls, and other public facilities.

The *danchi* is thus physically distinct from the surrounding environment. Its high concrete walls rise in well-disciplined ranks over the jumble of tile roofs, shops, and paddy fields of its surroundings. The first gleaming, modern communities that appeared on the horizon twenty years ago seemed to promise an entirely new and enviable style of life.

Danchi developments in Ōsaka, Japan. Above, aerial view of high-rise and duplex danchi in the Nagayoshi district (1969). Below, danchi residences in the Ikejima district. Photographs courtesy of the City of Ōsaka Planning Division of the Ōsaka Planning Bureau.

In 1965 the author began a study of the effects of *danchi* housing on family and community patterns, using structured and open-ended interviews, psychological tests, and participant observation. The study was done mainly in a *danchi* of 14,000 residents in a suburb of Osaka; but other Kōdan Jūtaku *danchi* in that vicinity and in Nagoya and a slum clearance housing project for poor families very near the target *danchi* were studied for control. The finished study (Kiefer, 1968) included intensive case materials from twenty families compiled over a year of observation.

DANCHI RESIDENTS

The residences of Kōdan Jūtaku *danchi* are viewed by their countrymen and by themselves as "modernistic" (*kindaiteki*) and "progressive" (*shimpoteki*) (*Nihon Jūtaku Kōdan*, 1972:90-91). Their income is slightly higher than that of the average urban wage earner, they are better educated than average, they have smaller families, and a high proportion work for large corporations (Kasamatsu, 1963). Most of them live in large development complexes near major cities, from which the household heads commute to work. These communities, which range in population from a few thousand to several hundred thousand, are typically built in a short period of time and thrown open for occupancy to anybody who can afford the rent and suffer the waiting period, which is typically many months.

A NEW COMMUNITY

The entrance procedure generally attracts a clientele which is quite homogeneous in age and social class and mostly unknown to each other on moving-in day. This means that the *danchi* at its birth as a community has no real social organization, no elite class from which leaders can be chosen, and no machinery for the development of resident self-government. On the other hand, there is a definite need for leadership. The creation of the *danchi* typically raises unforeseen problems in the local community--such as inadequate schools and transportation facilities, rising prices, and voting and tax problems. Responsibility for these problems is not always clearly defined. Often both the builder and the local community have to be dealt with effectively if the problems in the *danchi* are to be remedied. The early years of the *danchi*-as-a-community are open season on leadership. Strong

personalities tend to emerge as advocates of this or that reform, and these "self-government peddlers," as one Japanese
journalist (Nozawa, 1964) calls them, struggle to create widespread interest in reform and vie for stable power positions
in the community. In the absence of contest rules, the game
sometimes gets pretty hot.

APATHY AND COMMUNITY CONSCIOUSNESS

Related to the problem of finding leadership is the
phenomenon of general apathy toward community government and
toward cooperation between residents. Whereas the middle
class often plays an active leadership role in ordinary
Japanese communities, the efforts of would-be *danchi* leaders
to build "community consciousness" among their neighbors is
largely fruitless, as the great majority of the *danchi* residents are simply not joiners or leaders. The reasons for this
are complex. It appears reasonable to assume that the non-
communality of the typical *danchi* resident stems from a lack
of any stake in the future of the community. Since he hopes
to move out of the *danchi* either to a *danchi* in some other
city or to his own home some day, how can he sustain enthusi-
asm for community organizations? While this is undoubtedly
part of the story, it does not fully explain the difference
between the *danchi* dweller and other highly mobile middle-
class populations. Residents of communities such as Whyte's
Park Forest (Whyte, 1956) or Dobriner's Levittown (Dobriner,
1963) were in much the same state of temporariness as the
danchi dwellers, and yet by comparison they were veritable
gluttons for organization.

An obstacle to community mindedness specific to the
Japanese white-collar class is the salaryman (*sarariiman*)
who works in a highly structured social environment remote
from the community both in space and in values (Vogel, 1963).
The work environment makes much heavier demands on his time
and loyalty than does that of his American counterpart, due
to the fact that Japanese bureaucracies still retain an
ethos of personal dedication and self-sacrifice in the interest of group goals. A cursory look at a lower-class housing project in 1966 by the present author indicated that a
lack of strong involvement in groups outside the community was
partly responsible for a greater involvement on the part of
the lower-class husband in the affairs of the community. By
contrast, the absence of the middle-class *danchi* male from

his community is so conspicuous that it has earned him the title *geshukunin papa* ("lodger papa"), and his community it-self, *beddo taun* ("bed town").

The lack of a real and present common enemy can also be seen as the cause for the absence of general cooperative acti-vity within the *danchi*. When such an enemy did appear, as in the form of threatened rent hikes in 1970, the national Kodan Jūtaku Tenants' Association rallied to form the National Liai-son Council to Oppose Rent Hikes and was able to put pressure on the government. They succeeded in forestalling rent hikes on already occupied Housing Corporation dwellings in 1970, 1971, and 1972.

Perhaps the most interesting aspect of the political apathy of the typical *danchi* resident is the contrast between the *danchi* and the more traditional urban neighborhood. Both Dore's work (1958) and my own (1968) have indicated that tra-ditional urban neighborhoods tend to be class stratified, and that among the upper classes there is a sense of responsibility for the management of the community. By contrast the white-collar residents of the study *danchi* not only scoffed at the idea of their neighbors telling them how to run the community, but also considered the responsibility for leadership to rest outside the community--usually with local and national govern-ment or with the builder. This attitude was countered by local government officials who complained that they could never get cooperation from the leaderless *danchi* group.

SOCIAL ASPECTS

INFORMAL SOCIABILITY

In order to understand the political behavior of the *danchi* residents, we must look at patterns of informal social-izing. The self-sufficiency of the white-collar *danchi* family all but removes the necessity of associations based on economic sharing, such as are found in lower-class projects and in socioeconomically heterogeneous urban neighborhoods (*cf.* Dore, 1958). In fact, economic self-sufficiency is a point of honor with most *danchi* residents, and this leads to a social pattern more conspicuous in the *danchi* than anywhere else in Japan-- namely, keeping up with the Joneses.

Two aspects of the *danchi* environment seem to fan the flames of conspicuous consumption. The first is what Dobriner (1963) has labeled the "visibility principle." The *danchi* apartment exposes its tenants and their possessions to the community more than does the traditional Japanese home, cloistered within its walls and gardens. Looking up at the columns and rows of balconies on a typical *danchi* building, each festooned with the daily wash, it is tempting to compare the quality of socks and underwear. Second, there is the relative lack of grounds other than material ones by which to evaluate one's status in the community. This can be compared with similar findings by Young and Wilmott (1957), who noticed a sudden thirst for material possessions on the part of East Londoners who moved from the slums to a New Town in the suburbs--a thirst occasioned by the draining away of their non-material statuses: as the son of so-and-so, the fellow with the best jokes, or the one who had had a small moment of glory on such-and-such a memorable day. To most of its neighbors, the *danchi* family is known largely by appearances. This may be attributed to relative status deprivation of the upwardly mobile surrounded by upwardly mobiles.

The lack of formal structure and status hierarchy in the *danchi* community results in a great deal of latitude for individual self-expression in interpersonal relations. There are few effective means for enforcing community norms since privacy is generally respected and relationships tend to be shallow and easily terminated. In fact, there is little knowledge of what norms should be followed, if any, so that people rarely pressure one another to conform to explicit standards, and community ideals and goals are less obvious than personal ones. This state of affairs creates special problems for women, who must find guidelines for interaction in order to carry out their roles as mothers and wives and to satisfy their needs for sociability.

THE ROLE OF THE WOMAN

In an intricate study of the social relationships of a group of women in a white-collar Tōkyō *danchi* in 1961, Morioka Kiyomi (1968) discovered some interesting patterns. He found that informal sociability was particularly difficult for women with small children. Over half of the women interviewed who had children under three years of age, reported having *no* intimate friends or neighborhood relationships whatsoever.

Obviously, women with small children have less free time and less freedom of movement than those with no children or older children. Also, middle-class Japanese norms regarding ideal motherly and wifely behavior tend to condemn recreation and the pursuit of personal enjoyment for young mothers. Another factor may be the association between having young children and having a tight family budget. The mothers of babies are probably more often married to younger men with lower salaries than are the mothers of older children, and have many more necessary expenses than do non-mothers. The legendary isolation of the young mother in the *danchi*, coupled with a value system which puts tremendous emphasis on the grooming of children (from the cradle on) for success in the highly competitive education and job markets of the metropolis, has given rise to the term *ikuji noirōze* (child-rearing neurosis) to describe her cramped, anxious life.

Further analysis of Morioka's (1968) findings reveals an important pattern in *type* of informal social interaction: The higher the education and income of the woman, the more likely she is to associate with a) people in voluntary "circle activities" centering on educational and handicraft pursuits, b) friends living outside her neighborhood within the *danchi*, and c) friends living outside the *danchi*. Conversely, the lower a woman's education and family income, the more likely she is to have her intimate relationships restricted to her neighborhood. It would appear that the possession of these two commodities-- education and money--broadens the range of possible choice in informal relations.

However, the cultivation of purely voluntary relation- ships based on mutual interest seems to be a new pattern for young middle-class wives. The relative absence of an ethic of voluntary sociability can be gathered from the results of a study conducted in three large *danchi* in the early 1960s. Over 70% of both sexes preferred living in circumstances where it is possible to withdraw from neighbors, and almost that many preferred the anonymity of the *danchi* to more traditional communities for that reason (Takenaka, 1964:20). The observations from the present study confirm this characteristic, al- though Morioka infers from his data that informal socializing between women is on the increase.

Voluntary sociability is in fact growing among the *danchi* residents. Boredom has already been mentioned as a motive for seeking out others. The confining space and the great

reduction in housework characteristic of *danchi* living, leave
women with a good deal of free time and very limited ways of
spending it within their own homes. Many are literally driven
out of their solitude this way. Another very important factor
is the relatively high status of women in the *danchi*. Again,
the vast majority of *danchi* husbands commute to work outside
the neighborhood, so that during the day the *danchi* is a community of women. Much of the business of running the community, as well as the home, therefore falls on women's shoul-
ders. Furthermore, the *danchi* husband's status is typically
anchored in his office group, and he tends to leave his status
in his community up to his wife, or at least to remain aloof
from the status-seeking games mentioned above. As long as
she stays out of trouble, she is fairly free to associate with
whom she pleases. In this study (1965-66), only 10% of the
households contained kin of the husband or wife, while 83%
were nuclear families (Kiefer, 1968:43). Thus, it appears the
wife is not likely to be under the watchful eye of either a
parent or a parent-in-law.

Finally, the relative age and class homogeneity of the
danchi has a complex effect on patterns of association. Although it leads to status competition among neighbors, it also
multiplies the possibilities of forming relationships on the
basis of common interest and discourages patron-client relationships of the sort familiar in traditional rural communities and urban neighborhoods (see *e.g.*, Dore, 1958). The
physical environment, of course, provides some impetus for
the cultivation of mutual-interest relationships, since there
are few common facilities at the neighborhood level other than
stairwells, dust chutes, and playgrounds for small children.
Neighbors must seek each other out in order to form close ties.

FEMININE ROLES AND THE FAMILY

One index of social and political change in the *danchi*
is the role of the nuclear family in the value structure. Current folk sociology in Japan supports our data which indicate
that the nuclear family is gaining ground against other institutions, and one frequently hears such terms as "my-home-ism"
(*mai-hōmu-shugi*) and the familially focussed "leisure boom"
(*rējā būmu*). Unfortunately, there seem to be no solid historical data to document this trend among *danchi* dwellers.
Danchi informants of this study were asked questions about
the relative importance of family and job, family and community,

family and *ie* (extended patrilineal family), and family and friends, but the responses were highly idiosyncratic and there are no time-series data by which to plot trends.

If "my-home-ism" is on the rise in the *danchi* as folk-lore would have it, the twin reasons would appear to be: 1) the decline of community and *ie* authority, and 2) the relative power of wives whose main loyalty is to the nuclear family. It is interesting that in the study *danchi* many wives had begun to take active roles in such organizations as the Women's Association and the PTA, and through these organizations were beginning to challenge traditionally male-dominated institutions such as schools and city government. Typically, they justified this sort of "questionable" behavior in terms of their duties to their husbands and children. It is safe to say, at any rate, that the relative salience of the nuclear family in the *danchi vis à vis* both *personal-individual* goals and the status of other institutions is in a state of flux. It seems that "my-home-ism" might be an intermediate stage between the pre-metropolitan communal collectivist pattern and an ethic of stark individuality. Indeed, one hears more and more about *"ūman ribbu"* (women's lib), which perhaps signifies a transition toward the latter ethic.

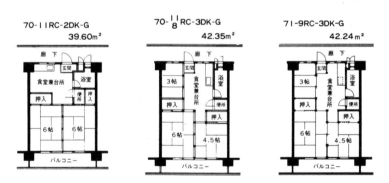

Three <u>danchi</u> floor plans offered in Ōsaka, Japan. These municipal apartments were offered in 1970, and have two-three rooms, dining room-kitchen, bathroom, and small storage area. The construction is reinforced concrete. Photo courtesy of Ōsaka City Planning Division of the Ōsaka City Planning Bureau.

THE *DANCHI* AND FUTURE POLITICS

There are, of course, many factors extrinsic to the
danchi community which affect its residents, and it is impossible to predict what effects local and national developments
will have on its political behavior. However, it seems likely
that the characteristics of *danchi* life described here will
exert some predictable influences on Japanese political behavior in a general way. These influences can be divided into
two types: 1) those affecting general characteristics of political participation, and 2) those affecting the content of
political values.

It seems likely that women will take an increasingly
active role in local, if not national, politics as a direct
result of *danchi* influences. They have more time, more responsibility, and relatively more authority than in traditional
sorts of neighborhoods; and they are, generally speaking, a
progressive and well-educated group.

The great latitude for choice regarding extent of political involvement in the *danchi* as compared with other communities, combined with transience and deracination, will probably
result in the spread of political apathy and cynicism at the
community level. When leadership is needed, contending ideological factions tend to spring up with the result that little
gets accomplished aside from the exchange of character defama-
tions. The average male resident will tend to identify with
his work colleagues and his family instead of his neighbors.
At the same time, residents may turn increasingly to metropolitan or national respresentatives and organizations for the
solutions for their increasingly supralocal problems.

However, the combination of the two factors--feminine
involvement and freedom of choice--may actually foster grass-
roots political action at both the municipal and national
levels in those cases where the issues appear to be immediate
and clear-cut, as in the case of rent hikes. If such should
be the case, then we can expect future Japanese politicians
to be more sensitive to the feminine vote and to the *danchi*
vote.

Turning to the area of political values, one possibility
is that the groups that are fostered by *danchi* life might become increasingly important as *loci* of political ideology.

It is possible that the increasing differences in behavior between the residents of class-homogeneous *danchi* and the surrounding populations will lead to an increase of class consciousness in the *danchi*. Also, both the nuclear family and the voluntary leisure-time group are likely to gain ground as sources of new political values. For example, there was a large car club in the study *danchi* which had succeeded in getting parking areas installed and some of the driving rules changed. Since the nuclear family thrives (at least theoretically) on leisure time for the breadwinner, *danchi* women may well be inclined to fight for things like shorter industrial and governmental working hours.

NEW ROLE MODELS

The effects on feminine values of increased autonomy and the increased need for self-reliance in interpersonal relationships with other women is complex, subtle, and long-term. They might turn out to be most important and result in a search for new sources of identity on the part of women--sources which are independent of the traditional roles of mother, daughter, wife, neighbor, and so on. These new sources of identity may be embraced much less because they represent performance of prescribed behavior, and much more because they embody personal ideals. Political conformity and even political practicality may become more and more uncommon among an increasing number of women. The necessity of constructing one's own social life on the basis of shared interests leads to increased self-consciousness, and, if successfully handled, to an increased sense of one's own ideas and ideals rather than collective mores and criteria of political rationality as a source of feelings of well-being.

If this is in fact going on, these views of the self will be communicated by young *danchi* mothers to their children of both sexes, and we can expect a bootstrapping of the process of individuation. What effects will this have on political behavior? One is tempted to look at the United States for examples, since the process seems to have gone further here, and the process may exert a conservative influence on American politics. For one thing, it leads to an emphasis on ideology at the expense of practical here-and-now issues, and ideology changes much more slowly than reality. For another thing, it leads, as David Riesman (1958) has pointed out, to diffuse "other-directedness" as the outcome of status competition and loneliness. When social status is cast loose from the moorings of kin and community, and when rules for evaluating performance become ambiguous, people are forced to look to very broad examples, such as those offered by the media, for standards by which to judge themselves. Combined with the trait of modern urbanites which Simmel (1902-03) called the "blasé attitude," the result is a lack of interest in political change.

PERSONAL MOBILITY AND POLITICS IN THE *DANCHI*

This paper has focused on the effects of some of the internal features of *danchi* life on politics. Let us now briefly consider the *danchi* as the expression of a nationwide problem --the housing problem. Kōdan *danchi* were created in order to allow the young married salaryman to live cheaply and save toward the universal middle-class dream--home ownership. The inflation of land and construction costs around the major cities has foiled this plan and trapped thousands of families in a style of life they wish to leave behind, and as a result the *danchi* has become a source of unrest.

Salarymen are quite sensitive to status indicators such as income and consumption habits, and the press keeps them supplied with a steady stream of national statistics against which they can measure themselves. Since so many *danchi* household heads are between 25 and 45 years old, it is not too difficult for a salaryman to accept *danchi* status during the early years of his marriage and career if he can continually reassure himself that he will graduate to home ownership by the time he has reached the age at which staying in the *danchi* might be a sign of failure. For most, the desire to escape the *danchi* environment is strong, for the *danchi* is a kind of status limbo--a symbol of halfway success that serves to whet the appetite for the payoff of the middle-class dream. Thus, one report on the Japanese housing situation (Kasamatsu, 1963) reports a *negative* correlation between the adequacy of housing as determined by objective standards of space and sanitation on one hand, and felt-satisfaction with housing on the other. A more recent report (*Nihon Jūtaku Kōdan*, 1972) shows that only 22% of a sample of 500 *danchi* wives wanted to stay in the *danchi* a long time and that more than half the sample actively disliked the term, "*danchi zoku*" (*danchi* dwellers).

Aside from the status implications of living in the *danchi*, there are other unpleasantries. The tenant feels helpless when facilities break down. Little attention is paid to upkeep on the buildings, either by tenants or management, and the *danchi* begins to take on a ragged look after a few years. With the standard of living rising, upwardly mobile families move out, and their place is often taken by people of humbler occupation and education. In order to escape this process of "slummation," some families give up their hopes for a real home, and move to newer, larger, more expensive *danchi*. This is, of course, no solution to the problem since the process will only be repeated in the newer *danchi*--and the chance to save toward a real home is even more remote because of the higher rent and the spiralling cost of living.

The current cooling off of the Japanese economy and leveling off of the standard of living increase may cause *danchi* residents to revise their priorities somewhat and to be satisfied with a secure status quo. If this happens, we might actually see a change toward greater interest in community political involvement and national measures to improve the quality of *danchi* life. If this does not happen, we can expect that the *danchi* residents will continue actively to seek personal and political solutions to the problems of home ownership.

CONCLUSION

This paper has suggested some of the processes of changing interpersonal behavior in the *danchi* that are likely to affect styles of political participation and contents of political attitudes, one way or another. It has also indicated how these styles of behavior are closely related to the history, economics, and physical ecology of the *danchi* community and to its place in Japanese society at large. There is little doubt that the *danchi* will continue to grow as a type of environment in Japan, and that we will have to watch closely the behaviors and attitudes associated with *danchi* living if we are to understand the future of Japanese politics.

REFERENCES

Dobriner, William M. *Class in Suburbia.* Englewood Cliffs, N.J.: Prentice-Hall, 1963.

Dore, R.P. *City Life in Japan.* Berkeley: University of California Press, 1958.

Kasamatsu Keiichi (ed.) *Danchi no Subete (All about Danchi).* Seikatsu Rigaku Chōsa Kai, 1963.

Kiefer, C.W. "Personality and Social Change in a Japanese *Danchi.*" Unpublished PH.D. Dissertation, University of California, Berkeley, 1968.

Morioka, Kiyomi. "Life History and Social Participation of Families in *Danchi,* Public Housing Project, in a Suburb of Tokyo." *International Christian University Journal of Social Science,* No. 7, 1968; reprinted in *Japan Institute of International Affairs Annual Review* (date unknown), pp. 92-158.

Nihon Jūtaku Kōdan. "'Sumi' ni kansuru Shufu no Ishiki Chōsa-- *Danchi, Apaato*" ("Survey of Wives' Perceptions of 'home': *Danchi* and Apartment"). Report published by *Nihon Jūtaku Kōdan,* May, 1972.

Nozawa Hiroshi. *Danchi.* Tōkyō: Shinjū Shoin, 1964.

Riesman, David. *The Lonely Crowd: A Study of the Changing American Character.* New Haven: Yale University Press, 1958.

Simmel, Georg. "The Metropolis and Mental Life." In *The Sociology of Georg Simmel.* Edited by K.H. Wolff. Glencoe, Ill.: The Free Press, 1950.

Takenaka Tsutomu. *Danchi Nanatsu no Daizai (The Seven Great Crimes of the Danchi).* Tōkyō: Kobundo Frontier Books, 1964.

Vogel, E.F. *Japan's New Middle Class.* Berkeley and Los Angeles: University of California Press, 1963.

Whyte, Wm. H. *The Organization Man.* Garden City, New York: Doubleday and Company, 1956.

Young, Michael, and Peter Wilmott. *Family and Kinship in East London.* London: Kegan-Paul, 1957.

III

THE IMPACT OF RAPID URBAN CHANGE ON NEIGHBORHOOD SOLIDARITY: A CASE STUDY OF A JAPANESE NEIGHBORHOOD ASSOCIATION

*G.R. Falconeri**

PERSPECTIVES

The late historian, Sir George B. Sansom, once wrote of his taste for "dynastic quarrels, political strife, treason, conspiracy, plots, battles, murders, and other public and private adventures and crimes" (1962:v). He realized these had gone out of fashion decades ago, yet to him they had remained as much the proper stuff of history as economic discourses and cultural trends. He preferred to view history not as a pageant but as "a motley procession with some bright banners but with many dingy emblems out of step and not very certain of its destination" (1962:vi).

Sansom was devoted also to the study of what the French have called *"la petite histoire*; of everyday life as it is lived ...by ordinary human beings who in their communities and societies make the raw material from which history is shaped" (Sansom, 1965:44). The following case study of a small Japanese neighborhood is but one example of a community caught up in the pageant

*G.R. Falconeri is an Associate Professor of East Asian History at the University of Oregon and currently Resident Director at the International Division of Waseda University in Tōkyō. The author wishes to acknowledge the beneficial association with Professors Willert Rhynsberger of Portland State University and Richard A. Smith of the University of Oregon, and to thank them for permission to use some of the charts and statistical tables which appear in this paper. Special words of appreciation go to the respective neighborhood association leaders and the residents of Saiwai-chō, Kanazawa City, Japan, and to officials of the Kanazawa municipal government. Much of this study is based on long hours of discussion with these patient people, observation of the changes in the area for over a decade, and the documentary resources provided by various persons and groups involved in the changes that have taken place there. Grateful thanks are extended to the Social Science Research Council for a summer research grant and to the University of Oregon's Institute of International Studies for allowing me to lead a group of young American students to Kanazawa for interdisciplinary field research.

31

of modernization. This neighborhood may be considered one of those dingy emblems as it is forced to cope with "public and private adventures and crimes" upon its being for which it was not prepared, and in which the pressure of change has caused increasing uncertainty about the community's identity and destination.

To place this study in perspective, I will begin with a brief comment on how the study of modernization has attracted researchers.

TOWARD DEFINING MODERNIZATION

In the summer of 1960 at Hakone, scholars in the first Conference on Modern Japan struggled to find an acceptable definition of modernization. One dynamic approach to understanding modernization that was advanced was based on the concept that it is "the process by which historically evolved institutions are adapted to the rapidly changing functions that reflect the unprecedented increase in man's knowledge, permitting control over his environment, that accompanied the scientific revolution" (Black, 1960:7). This adaptation to rapid change is a key factor in clarifying the complex phenomenon of modernization, but in terms of the impact of modernization on human communities, it is equally important to take note of instances of *non*-adaptation by the "historically evolved institutions" which give coherence and meaning to community life. The case of the neighborhood association of Saiwai-chō in Kanazawa City is one such instance.

In Japan's case, modernization has been generally viewed as a march which first traversed the geographic area encompassing the feudal Tōkaidō (Eastern Sea Road) from Edo (Tōkyō) southwest to Kyōto, continuing along the Pacific Ocean and Inland Sea coasts of Honshū down through Western Kyushu. Today, the entire nation--and particularly its metropolitan core zones--is characterized by a "high degree of urbanization and relatively highly organized forms of government" (Almond and Coleman, 1960:52). There is "an extensive and penetrative network of mass communication [and] the existence of large-scale social institutions such as government, business, and industry and the increasing bureaucratic organization of such institutions" (Jansen, 1965:19).

Yet much of our attention is drawn to such overarching aspects of modernization as industrialization, governmental institution-building, and metropolitanization, as well as to the

unfortunate concomitants of rapid social and economic moderniza-
tion--those problems such as crowding, pollution, traffic congestion, and the like, which often appear to us as universal to
modern nations but are particularly acute in Japan. Perhaps in
our rush to deal with the "big picture" and its concomitant problems, we have neglected some other aspects of the modernization
process that we should have looked at more closely. As an example, one often-held assumption is that "modernization is accompanied by a movement in society from Gemeinschaft to Gesellschaft
conditions" (Maruyama and Bellah, as reported in Jansen, 1965:27).
However, studies of individual urban neighborhoods where *gemeinschaft* orientations have undergone, or are still undergoing,
transmutation into *gesellschaft* form have not attracted much of
our attention. They have become, like Sansom's battles and con-
spiracies, "old fashioned." Still, we might learn from these
late changing communities and their institutions more about the
process of modernization and how it affects institutions and
practices that are still with us but which hark back to an earlier stage of development. One variant of this perspective is to
learn why *gemeinschaft* institutions adapt, or fail to adapt, to
rapidly changing circumstances around them.

BY-PRODUCTS OF MODERNIZATION

More important perhaps than refining theories, we might
seek in these "outdated" organizations and practices how to avoid
some of the ugly by-products of modernity. For example, the
search for earlier mechanisms of cooperation to solve urban problems appears to be one of the causes behind the recent dramatic
rise of neighborhood groups in the United States. Certainly in
Japan the forms of social solidarity so prevalent in traditional
villages and towns and carried over into urban settings have had
their share of successes in coping with myriad problems over a
long time.

Nevertheless, today we see that a delicate balance of neighborhood well-being is endangered by the twin juggernauts of rapid
urbanization and industrialization which the fragile *gemeinschaftlich* institutions and practices are often powerless to resist.
Unfortunately, the tyranny of these changes does not affect institutions only--it affects people as well. It tests the degree
to which the individual and the family will sacrifice for what
they have been told is the general good. Moreover, it often
places those who have been involved over the longest periods of
time in the local processes of mutual self-help in an abhorrent
condition of encirclement by strange newcomers and dependence on
higher political authority. It prevents these people from playing

any sort of meaningful, autonomous role either on their own behalf or as participants in community cooperative ventures with
their neighbors.

The upshot is that the neighborly milieu where public and
private considerations have often meshed for the community good
is now pervaded by a social ennui where self-interest and community disinterest may prevail. Under such conditions neighbors may conclude that such local organizations as the *chōnaikai* (or *chōkai*, neighborhood association) are no longer effective in maintaining social cohesion and neighborhood identity,
or in resisting the power of municipal, prefectural, and national
authorities should these higher agencies make demands on the
neighborhood that are considered disadvantageous to the residents
of the area. The result is that so long as the *chōnaikai* remains
free of major challenges, it can continue to expect a modest participation from the neighborhood. Once tested and found incapable
of asserting itself in the interests of its members, the *chōnaikai*
becomes vulnerable.

This may be inevitable for such fragile organizations. Perhaps only in situations where the need for neighborhood solidarity
is paramount--as in Belfast where Roman Catholic Clonard and Prot-
estant Woodvale have based their values and existence on maintaining the integrity of the neighborhood with paramilitary organiza-
tion--will we see the vitality of areal organization at its highest
level. But seldom is the enemy so clearly defined and immediately
confronted as in these Irish neighborhoods. In many instances
"modernity" is faceless and not viewed as an enemy until too late.
Indeed, in Japan modernity--however defined--is welcomed; and its
pursuit, especially since the end of World War II, has overwhelmed
many efforts to retain older forms of local organization. This
is especially true if such older forms are deemed "bothersome" by
the bureaucratic powers of the modern state. Nostalgic, perhaps
naive, concerns for the old neighborhood as a good place to grow
up and live, where one can talk over problems and pleasantries
with neighbors out on the stoop give way to considerations of
rationalization for efficiency's sake. The standards set elsewhere for the neighborhood, the family, and the individual often
place primacy on the benefits to be derived by the nation, the
prefecture, and the municipality. The trade-off invariably is
couched in terms of "the general good," but the local residents
may feel they have given up much more than they have received.

CHANGING NEIGHBORHOOD INSTITUTIONS

The *chōnaikai*, a product of Japanese village orientations
carried over into the urban setting, was partially fostered by

feudal sumptuary laws which forced families of similar status and occupation into particular neighborhoods and inevitably created communities of common interest. Having served the residents as well as the administrative authorities of villages, towns, and cities as liaisons, the *chōnaikai* served a critical function in the administration of the feudal domain, and later the prefecture and the nation. Like Janus, they looked in two directions and in effect served two masters. In prewar days the *chōnaikai* were nongovernmental associations staffed by unpaid volunteers, which became an efficient and inexpensive arm of the Japanese government. During the war they provided indispensable service as police, civil defense, and rations distribution agencies, among other functions. Despite their association with Japan's wartime cause and close ties with the military, as well as efforts by the United States Occupation authorities to eradicate them, *chōnaikai* continued into the postwar years. War may have changed their activities but not the need for such groups as agents of neighborhood solidarity. However, with the striking upsurge of rural to urban migration since World War II and the political and sociological changes this phenomenon has brought about,[1] it proved frequently impossible to maintain in old neighborhoods and to create in new ones the solidarity so essential to the achievement of local needs.

It is with the problems of neighborhood solidarity and the struggle to prevail in the face of overwhelming change that this paper is concerned. The study focuses on two pervasive changes that have occurred over the past ten years in one particular neighborhood in Kanazawa, a medium size city near the Japan Sea coast. The first of the changes was the dissection of the community by a major arterial, and the second the formation of a modern administrative liaison system that largely replaced the older community organizations. Most observers would consider the first of the changes rather commonplace. This factor itself is significant as it suggests the fragility of local organizations when confronted by higher authority and also because of the frequency of similar events in other Japanese cities. Both changes have had a debilitating and possibly fatal effect on the solidarity of this neighborhood.

The first of the changes, the arterial construction, is known as the Mitsukuchi project and dissects the neighborhood

---

[1] Examples of such changes are the growth of danchi (high rise apartment complexes), large industrial concentrations, nonlocal leisure activities, and a general impersonality of life. For an interesting statistical study of rural to urban migration in the 1960s, see Keiichi Takeuchi, "The Rural Exodus in Japan: Basic Considerations for International Comparison," *Hitotsubashi Journal of Social Studies*, Vol. 7 (April, 1974), pp. 17-38, and Vol. 8 (May, 1976), pp. 35-47.

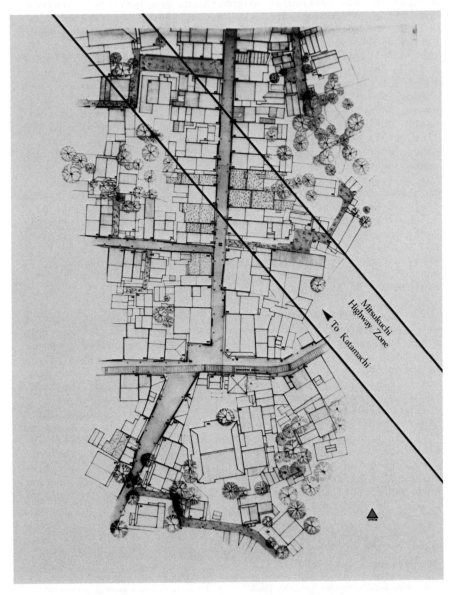

FIGURE 1.　BUILDING MASS DRAWING OF SAIWAI-CHŌ STREET CENTER
SHOWING MITSUKUCHI HIGHWAY DISSECTION (*Drawing
courtesy of Richard A. Smith, University of Oregon*)

into two unequal parts (see Figure 1). The second change, an
administrative innovation being watched by other cities in Japan,
is the implementation of a new system of administrative liaison
between the municipal government and individual families throughout the city. While the experience of this one *chōnaikai* may be
repeated in many neighborhoods in Japan, it would be naive to
suggest that from this case we can come to understand the com-
plexities of the interaction of *gemeinschaftlich* organizations
and rapid urban change. Rather it is the objective of this
study to provide a historical description based on an intermit-
tent observation of one small community facing its problems.
The neighborhood could be one of Sansom's dingy emblems--out of
step with modernization, fighting a losing battle, being brought
into step, and, at least for now, not so certain of its destination.

THE CASE OF SAIWAI-CHŌ

HISTORICAL SETTING

Located just a short distance from the Sai River in the
heart of the old castle town of Kanazawa, Saiwai-chō has enjoyed
a long and varied history. Saiwai-chō is a classic case of
Ishida Takeshi's caveat regarding the generalization that all
neighborhood solidarity is based on old village forms. Its population was largely composed of farmers who became members of the
"old middle class, such as shopkeepers, who have lived and worked
in the same place for generations" (Ishida, 1971:57). Originally
the town sprang up along a country road leading to hunting
grounds of the wealthy Maeda lord and his chief deputy family,
the Honda. The main street stretched from the entrance of the im-
pressive Keikaku-ji Buddhist Temple to a watercourse beyond which
lay the older *samurai* (warrior) residential area of Honda-machi.
Its boundaries are easily identified. Physically, the area is
reminiscent of a typical temple town in Japan. Yet there is a
singular lack of religious goods shops now. Despite the Keikaku-
ji Temple's presence in the area before Saiwai-chō was formed,
it has not dominated the town's development. Rather, the impetus
for its formation and growth came from its association with the
feudal castle town. The original shopkeepers, over time, increased their mercantile activities by providing for the daily
necessities of the warrior families of the adjacent town of Honda-
machi. Their shops and homes formed the nucleus of the old town.
For several centuries the line of residences fronted by shops
along this street center was known as Hyakusho-machi (Farmers'
Town).

Eventually, the street center and the houses surrounding it came to be incorporated into a neighborhood within the growing and expanding city of Kanazawa, and a strong sense of identity was developed. The shops prospered and Saiwai-cho became a small district shopping center still offering commodities for daily life. (See Figure 2.) By 1965 the local *chōnaikai*, called the Hyakushinkai, was composed of approximately 208 families divided into fourteen sections *(rinpō han)*. While there was the usual movement of families in and out of the area, the number of households has remained relatively stable over the past two generations. Changes in the composition of the neighborhood (in this case specifically referring to the area of the Hyakushinkai *chōnaikai*) result from births and deaths, out-migration of young residents, and from marriages. Land is at a premium in Japanese cities and such is the case in Saiwai-cho. High-rise apartments have not been built in the area to date. Most new families, therefore, tend to be the products of marriages of sons who have brought their brides to live either in their parents' house or, more likely nowadays, in a small apartment built at the back of whatever land might be held by the senior family. Most young families prefer to live separately from parents and this small apartment arrangement is a compromise which appears to be meeting the modern concerns of the new family as it does the more traditional considerations of the older generation. It also links the younger generation to the community.

In 1965, in addition to the *chōnaikai*, there was a shopkeepers' association *(shōtenkai)* which numbered thirty-two members. It was affiliated with a regional urban shopkeepers' league and, by extension, to the Kanazawa City Chamber of Commerce. Because many of the families were also shopkeepers, the activities of the *chōnaikai* and *shōtenkai* tended to involve many of the same people; as would be expected, however, the shopkeepers' association concerned itself exclusively with the business problems of its thirty-two members.

POLITICAL ORGANIZATION

The Hyakushinkai, like other *chōnaikai* in Kanazawa, belongs to the Kanazawa City League of Neighborhood Associations *(Kanazawa Chōnaikai Rengōkai;* see Figure 3). Unlike some of the more affluent and politically active *chōkai*, the Hyakushinkai is not particularly involved in the affairs of the League. It pays its annual dues, sends its representative to the League's infrequent meetings, and provides the League with the usual reports on its finances, household registers, census statistics, and other matters that are part of the reporting procedures for the *chōnaikai*

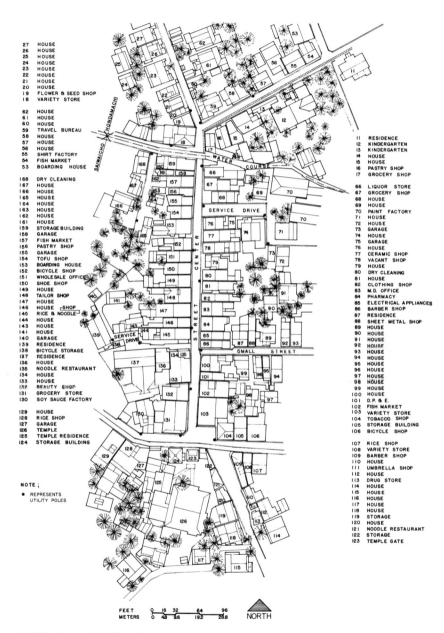

FEET   0 16 32   64   96
METERS 0 4.8 9.6 19.2 28.8   △ NORTH

FIGURE 2. SPATIAL INVENTORY OF NEIGHBORHOOD FACILITIES (courtesy
of Richard A. Smith, University of Oregon)

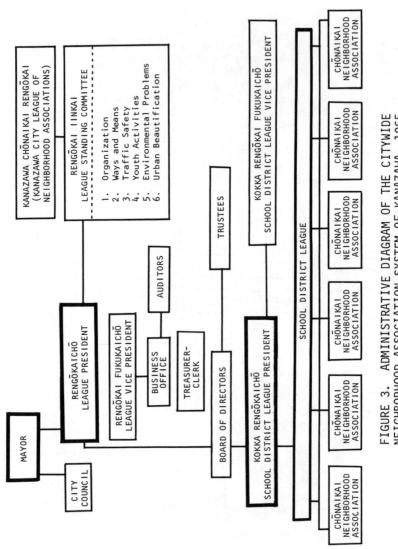

FIGURE 3. ADMINISTRATIVE DIAGRAM OF THE CITYWIDE
NEIGHBORHOOD ASSOCIATION SYSTEM OF KANAZAWA, 1965

in the city. Through the League it does enjoy the right to appeal to a larger, more influential body for assistance when it
cannot resolve problems directly with the proper municipal authorities. Generally speaking, this sort of recourse to the League
has been successful only when a number of *chōnaikai* share the
same problem and the municipal authorities are in some agreement
that the issue at hand should be solved in the general interest of the city. In brief, the League can and does act on behalf of a number of *chōnaikai* if an adversary relationship should
develop with the municipal authorities but it usually strives to
bring about compromise and consensus. Seldom does it act where
the interests of only one *chōnaikai* are concerned.

More often than not, if the *chōnaikai* must seek outside assistance beyond its direct appeals to the city hall it does so
through the group of *chōnaikai* with which it is associated in
its school district. Throughout the city the *chōnaikai* are divided into groups according to the school district to which they
belong. Since the welfare of the children of the neighborhoods
is an important part of the overall consideration of the *chōnaikai*, close liaison is maintained with the school district leaders.
The Hyakushinkai has had a long history of exemplary attention
to the needs of the residents of the neighborhood and has taken
seriously its responsbilities toward the school district and
the municipal government. (See Figure 4.)

In 1965 the *chōnaikai* head (*chōkaichō* or *chōnaikaichō*) was
a Mr. Wada,[2] a man in his late forties, a middle school principal
whose family had long been carpenters. His association with the
chō and the schools was thought to be advantageous for the residents of Saiwai-cho. His wife, he jokingly reported, did most
of the *chōnaikai* work, while he reaped most of the credit. Mr.
Wada conducted the monthly meetings of the Hyakushinkai and acted
as the representative of the *chō* to lateral and higher authorities. His primary function as he saw it was to maintain harmony
among the residents, plan for future developments in the neighborhood, maintain a sanitary neighborhood environment, and carry on
the routine of the Hyakushinkai. Mrs. Wada was head of the
women's auxiliary (*fujinbu*) of the Hyakushinkai, head of the subdivision (*hanchō*) in which the Wada family lived, and an ad-
visor to the children's group (*kodomakai*) of the *chō*. The Wadas'
son and daughter belonged to the youth group (*seinenbu*). In addition, Mrs. Wada would keep track of persons moving into and
leaving the *chō*, keep the list of names of residents up-to-date,
remind families of special events, greet newcomers to the *chō*,
bid farewell to those departing, and carry messages, reports, and

---

[2] All personal names have been changed.

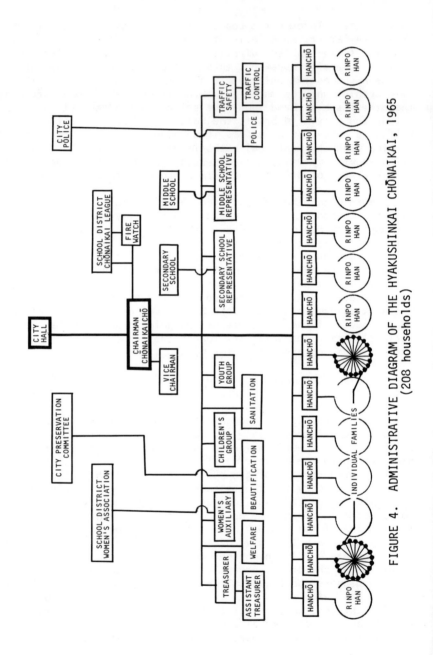

FIGURE 4.   ADMINISTRATIVE DIAGRAM OF THE HYAKUSHINKAI CHŌNAIKAI, 1965
(208 households)

other matters of routine business to the proper departments in
the city offices. Her tasks were of a varied nature and she
served as the "face" of her husband, the *chōnaikai* head. Mr.
Wada thought of himself as the idea man. It was he who per-
suaded the residents of the *chō* to change the name from Hyakusho-machi (Farmers' Town) to Saiwai-cho (literally, Happy or
Happiness Town).

The vice-chairman of the *chōnaikai* was Mr. Tanaka, a
dynamic man who owned the largest business in the *chō*, a supermarket and a beer, *sake*, and liquor distributorship located directly across from the Keikaku-ji temple. Mr. Tanaka was also
head of the *shōtenkai* and as such wielded considerable influence
in Saiwai-cho. In 1965, Mrs. Wada was succeeded by Mrs. Tanaka
as head of the women's auxiliary. Since Tanaka's businesses were
located in the heart of the *chō*, the couple was quite visible and
carried out many of the daily functions of the *chōnaikai*. When
Mr. Wada was forced to give up his leadership of the *chōnaikai*
owing to the Mitsukuchi project, Mr. Tanaka succeeded him as *chō-*
naikaichō. Had this construction not taken place, it is quite
probable that Mr. Wada would have continued to serve as *chōnai-*
kaichō for perhaps another year or two.[3]

THE HYAKUSHINKAI *KAIRANBAN* (CIRCULATING INFORMATION BOARD)[4]

World, national, and regional news in Japan are amply reported by the media, but for news pertinent to the immediate
neighborhood the Japanese have for centuries used a circulating
board. This is usually nothing more than a clipboard with notices
or information considered important to *chō* residents. It is accompanied by a list of all the families in the *rinpo-han*. The *kairan-*
ban usually emanates from the *chōnaikai* head. The *hanchō* sees that
it goes to the next door neighbor's house where it is expected that
either the husband or wife (usually the latter) will read it and pass
on the information to other members of the family. Once having read
the notice, the family seal is affixed and the circulating board is
passed on immediately to their next door neighbor. Families in
the Hyakushinkai are prompt in reading and circulating the board
according to both Mr. Wada and Mr. Tanaka. If a neighbor is out
of town or known to be unable to circulate the board promptly,
that house is bypassed and returned to after the board has made

---

[3]There was no fixed length of time in Saiwai-cho for tenure in office. By custom,
the usual length of time was three years. In the neighboring chō of Shimo Honda-machi,
the chōnaikaichō had been in office for more than ten years. Throughout the city, terms
of office vary.

[4]See Appendix A for a summary of entries on the Hyakushinkai kairanban from early
in April to late in July, 1965. The term machi used in these entries corresponds to the
term chō as used in this narrative.

the rounds back to the house of the *hanchō* and then to the *chōnai-kai* head. In most instances one of the children of the *chōnaikai-chō* will take the circulating board to those families whose seals do not appear on the board. The process is fast and efficient and continues to be used in many neighborhoods in rural and urban Japan.

In the spring and summer of 1965, the Hyakushinkai *kairanban* covered a number of the usual topics: meetings, announcements, appreciation for donations to charities, school activities, con-dolences for deaths in the *chō*, reports from the school district and city offices, notices of the youth group's successful parti-cipation in the school district volleyball league, plans for a trip of the older residents for an excursion to the nearby Noto peninsula, and announcements regarding the availability and proper use of insecticides for controlling summer insects and pests. There were a number of entries cautioning children to work toward keeping the *chō* clean and exhorting them to parti-cipate in the periodic cleanup campaigns on weekends. Traffic notices were always to be found in the circulating board. Since the traffic down the street center of Saiwai-cho was always of a high density, this was a high priority concern. Accidents did occur from time to time but owing to the tight quarters and narrowness of the streets, automobile speeds were restricted and accidents tended to be minor. At times a shopkeeper's "Coca Cola" or "*Sake*" sign might be damaged, but serious injury or death was almost unheard of in the area.

The area encompassed by the Hyakushinkai was crowded but clean and vibrant. It had a rhythm of life which saw the street occupied by different segments of the neighborhood at different times during the day. In the early morning hours the older women could be seen with short-handled brooms and dust pans sweeping the area in front of their houses and clearing out the foot-wide water trough that travelled the length of the street on each side. Afterward came commuters on their way to work; then the hordes of students who passed through the main street en route to the junior and senior high schools adjacent to the *chō*. Stores and shops would begin to open for business, and delivery trucks as well as garbage and "honey bucket" trucks would invade the street. In Saiwai-cho there were very few houses with flush toilet facili-ties and these "honey bucket" trucks with their long suction hoses for cleaning out the holding tanks in the houses were a common sight--and smell. For years there was talk of coordinating the schedule of these trucks but nothing ever came of it. In the hot afternoons Saiwai-cho appeared to slumber. A few preschool children might be seen seated on a straw mat or two, playing in a doorway or on the side of the narrow street or in a side street. From around four in the afternoon activity began to increase as

housewives began to do their daily shopping, merchants began
hawking their products, students began to clutter the streets
on their way home, and in brief, a high pitch of activity moved
into full swing for the next two hours or so. From around six-
thirty to nine in the evening, the streets were peopled by
various family members casually window shopping, talking to one
another or to the shopkeepers, who were beginning to tidy up
their shops and prepare for the next day. Commuters would be
seen coming home from a hard day at the office or factory. After
ten at night the streets became quiet and generally dark, lighted
at intervals by the street lamps provided through an arrangement
between the city offices and the Hyakushinkai. Only an occasional
male would be seen as he wound his way home after having imbibed
a bit too much. Throughout the night the *chōnaikai* fire watch,
a male member of the family whose turn it was to do the job,
could be heard as he clacked together the two hardwood sticks
while he made his rounds. Only this reassuring sound announcing
that all was well disturbed the sleeping neighborhood.

Residents of the Hyakushinkai often dreamed of living up
on Izumi-no-machi hill where the more affluent in the city resided
in larger houses with more space and gardens and where the streets
were broader and the neighborhood a bit more quiet. Still, they
recognized that they were one link in a line of generations who
had lived in the same houses on this same street. There was a
quiet sense of pride in their *chō* just as all residents of Kanazawa seemed to have a sense of pride from living in the once-
great castle town of the Maeda lords. They realized that their
sons and daughters would probably leave for work in other cities,
but they also expected that at least one of their children would
remain in Saiwai-chō to continue the family's tradition and the
neighborhood's link with the past.

There were two other entries on the circulating board in
the spring and summer of 1965 that were not of the usual sort.
One was of little consequence and merely notified the residents
of the *chō* of a small group of faculty and students from the
United States who planned to study the area and make some architectural drawings of the temple and houses. The other mentioned
a meeting that the *chōnaikai* head and vice-chairman had had with
the City Planning Office about some urban renewal plans.

Central to the city's development plan was the construction
of a major four-lane highway to connect the downtown areas of
Katamachi and Korinbo with the national highway network and outlying suburban communities. The new highway would cut a free
flowing traffic channel through the chaotic street pattern of the
city, a legacy of Kanazawa's feudal past when the streets were

planned and constructed to meet the defensive needs of the castle
and to stifle movement. Indeed, some young men in the Planning
Office joked that it was a shame that Kanazawa, unlike Toyama, her
sister city to the north, had not been bombed during World War II
so that city fathers could reconstruct along the modern grid pattern as did other cities.

Planners appealed to the business sense of the *shōtenkai*
leaders. They emphasized that a number of the Saiwai-cho shops
would benefit from the arterial construction and that they
would be able to transport their goods downtown to Katamachi and
Korinbo where nighttime entertainment businesses would need the
food and other items prepared in Saiwai-cho. They appealed to
the expansionist tendency of these small entrepreneurs but they
neglected to point out, or conveniently chose to ignore, the
fact that this was a neighborhood shopping center and its customers had been drawn largely from the families in the immediate
surrounding areas within walking or bicycling distance. This
meant there would be a potential loss of business as housewives
and youths would gain easy access by bus to the more inviting
department stores, the many variety shops in Katamachi, and the
huge fish and vegetable market in Musashi-ga-tsu-ji just beyond
Korinbo.

PROGRESS: THE COMMUNITY'S VISION

At first Mr. Tanaka and others in the *shōtenkai* welcomed
the idea of the Mitsukuchi thoroughfare development. They had
been planning to cover the main shopping street with a plastic
or metal canopy to protect shoppers during the heavy rains that
beset Kanazawa in the spring and autumn. One of the shopping
centers near Musashi-ga-tsu-ji had done so and had become very
crowded, busy, and lucrative for the shops there. Little thought
was given to the fact that Musashi-ga-tsu-ji itself drew shoppers
because of the department store and the fish and vegetable market
and that it was only a stone's throw from the shopping center on
which some Saiwai-cho merchants thought they might pattern their
chō after. While no one in the *shōtenkai* entertained the thought
that Saiwai-cho would become another Musashi-ga-tsu-ji, there
was talk of drawing shoppers to Saiwai-cho because of the new
access the arterial would afford. All attention was focused on
the potential attraction of new shoppers to--not loss of old
customers from--the area.

In *chōnaikai* meetings it was argued that the arterial would
relieve traffic congestion. This appealed to virtually all residents. Mr. Tanaka became especially active in championing the

Mitsukuchi project, talking with his neighbors and maintaining a
regular shuttle between the city planning office and Saiwai-chō.
Along with Mr. Wada, he sought to serve as the go-between in
discussions with *chō* residents and city officials. He expressed
sympathy for those families who might be displaced, but he saw
the plan as one that would contribute to the well-being of the
whole of Saiwai-chō. In fact, many of the problems that arose
were linked to the dispossession of some families from their
homes and shops. Other problems involved jealousies that developed between those who were forced to give up their land and those
who would benefit financially because of the location of their
properties near the new thoroughfare. No sooner had the plan become known than land values began to rise--some phenomenally.
Mr. Wada, the *chōnaikai* head, was directly in the path of the
construction. There was no alternative for him but to sell his
house and land to the government and move out to the suburbs
where land prices had been rising very rapidly. The move was no
boon to him despite the fact that he had received a reasonable
recompense for the inconvenience caused him and his family. His
residency in the *chō* having been broken, he gave up his post to
Mr. Tanaka.

The scramble caused by the Mitsukuchi project took several
forms. For those who, like Mr. Wada, were in the direct path of
destruction there was nothing that could be done. Interestingly
for a society where compromise and accommodation are hallmarks
of decision making, there did occur the sort of individualism so
often lauded in the United States. Mrs. Urakawa, a war widow,
staunchly held to her property rights as she sat in her Tokugawa
house. She was an island of last-ditch resistance as the giant
smashing ball and the bulldozer destroyed the other buildings
around her. Numerous city officials visited her home bearing
gifts in an effort to coax her into voluntarily leaving her home.
She remained for a year as the construction continued. But in
the end, she, too, fell to the weight of progress and sold out.

Others who were partially in the path of destruction resorted to a practice also visible in older crowded cities and along
village roads where buildings hug the streets. They simply lopped
off one of the corners of the house or shop and formed a triangular
structure. Often a second or a third floor was added from funds
received for the lost land, the living quarters moved upstairs,
and the shop extended further back on the first floor. It is
interesting to note that almost everyone argued with city planners to have the highway pass just a few feet to the right or
left of their property lines. Those who were forced to move or
who wished to move were offered special waivers to the usually
long waiting period for vacancies in apartment complexes. To

our knowledge no one chose this option. Finally, there was a
scramble by some of the more well-to-do in the area as well as
by business firms and wealthy people from outside to buy land
located along the route of the new arterial. Some succeeded in
convincing residents to sell part of their lots and in this way
were able to gain a foothold in the future business of the area.
One *sake* and liquor wholesaler, learning at an early planning
stage of the proposed construction, came into Saiwai-cho offering
to buy, at what seemed at the time abnormally high prices, the
land of several families located at the edge of the newly proposed construction. His offers triggered a wave of concern among
residents who feared they were not being told everything by city
authorities, but nothing occurred to stimulate actual opposition
to the project.

THE REALITY OF PROGRESS

        After much activity and delay the arterial was completed.
By 1972 the last potholes were filled, manhole covers put in
place, new buildings along the highway constructed, and the area
was trying to reconstitute itself. Some of the key figures in
the drama were gone from the scene. (See Table 1 for a list of
structural changes.) Mr. Wada was in the suburbs. Mr. Tanaka
had died unexpectedly of heart failure; his supermarket was closed
and his liquor and beer distributorship, much reduced in size, was
being operated by his son. The shopping street is now dissected
with one-third of the *chō* on one side of the arterial and two-
thirds on the other. Although only nine dwellings were completely destroyed along the old street center, it is important for our
purposes to note that more than half of those buildings in the
core area have changed their functions. Numerous other buildings
in the area--and we must bear in mind that we are concerned with
families in virtually all of these cases because of the dual
functions of buildings as residences and businesses--have also
had their uses changed. The problem of traffic congestion has
been relieved only slightly while along the highway even greater
traffic hazards prevail. Saiwai-cho has traded some of its neighborhood traffic problems (*e.g.*, narrow, crowded streets) for the
speed, exhaust fumes, and traffic jams endured by residents of
large cities.[5]

        Mr. Fuji, the new *chōnaikai* head following the death of
Mr. Tanaka, laments the passing of old Saiwai-cho not only because he considers it to have been a much better place in which
to live but also from his vantage point as a neighborhood official. He says the highway has become a barrier. Older residents

-----

[5]For a discussion of transport and housing in Japan, see Ursula Hicks, The Large
City: A World Problem (New York: Macmillan Co., 1974), pp. 198-208.

TABLE 1

STRUCTURAL CHANGES, 1965–1972

Buildings	Street Center		Outside of Street Center		Total	
	Number of buildings	%	Number of buildings	%	Number of buildings	%
Existing, 1965	39	100	92	100	131	100
Destroyed in Mitsukuchi Project	7	18	9	10	16	12
Existing, 1972	32	82	83	90	115	88
Changed in Function, 1972	15	38	10	11	25	19
Function in 1972 Unchanged from 1965	17	44	74	79	90	69
Total Destroyed or Changed between 1965 and 1972	22	56	19	21	41	31

Courtesy of Professor Willert Rhynsberger, Portland State University.

fear crossing it and youths and children have defied death every
day since its completion. In one week in 1972, shortly after the
highway went into use, two people were killed on the arterial.
By the summer of 1973, there had been thirteen serious accidents
which caused hospitalization or outpatient treatment. Mr. Fuji
talked of the fact that the thoroughfare had been built on what
was once a cemetery of the Keikaku-ji temple. In traditional
fashion, the temple priest was asked by the *chōnaikai* just after
the fatal accidents to offer prayers for the protection of the
spirits of the dead and to cleanse the area of those spiritual
elements which cause injury and death. According to Mr. Fuji
there had been no deaths or serious accidents since then, but
he is not at all sanguine that such practices as the Keikaku-ji
prayers will continue to have this salutary effect on the acci-
dent rate.

THE CHANGING FACE OF SAIWAI-CHŌ: SOCIAL AND POLITICAL

Physically, Saiwai-chō has been transformed from a discrete
lane with its shops, people, and vehicles mingled in close quarters into a nondescript residential-shopping area dominated by
the highway whose prime purpose is to link the center of the
city with outlying districts. Saiwai-chō is located along the
route of an arterial that was built for purposes that had little
to do with this neighborhood. Some new shops have been constructed on the arterial, but these are generally "quality shops"
directed toward the more affluent who drive by in their automobiles. *Haute couture* women's wear salons, automobile accessory
shops, and the like have moved into what was the outer fringe
of Saiwai-chō, and become a main shopping focus. Physically,
the neighborhood has opened up as anticipated by city planners
but the hopes of many in the *chōnaikai* and *shōtenkai* have not
materialized. The sense of community seems gone. Shoppers who
previously relied almost exclusively on the local shops for their
daily needs now often make their way downtown to the Katamachi
and Musashi-ga-tsu-ji department stores and shops where the
variety of goods is larger and the conveniences of shopping much
greater. Some, by dint of habit and a certain sense of loyalty
continue to shop in the "old town." Over the years this has
come to mean that the older housewives shop nearer home, while
the younger housewives often spend one or two afternoons downtown shopping.

For shop owners the change has had varying effects. From
interviews with these shopkeepers, it appears that only the *tōfu*
(bean cake) maker and the doctor continue much as before. The
shoe store is gone. The fish dealer, the barber shop, and other

small shops are having a very difficult time surviving, and many
of the men have taken other jobs while the women manage the
shops. Since the construction of a chain-type supermarket along
the highway a few short steps from the old street center, a number of the shops previously selling canned goods and other small
daily provisions have been suffering drastic decreases in sales.
The paint store and the umbrella store have been converted into
storage buildings, other small buildings may be seen housing
motorcycles and small automobiles behind the glassed sliding
doors where previously a small shop did its business. Even the
Keikaku-ji temple has given over some of its courtyard space
previously used as a community playground to automobile and
small-truck parking. Whereas before the highway came, Saiwai-chō
had no space for parking and few cars could be stopped for any
length of time, now the area has become a parking place with
parking spaces having replaced what was once a home or a shop.

Socially, the *chō* has undergone considerable adjustment.
Perhaps the most vivid evidence of the breakdown of neighborhood
solidarity is to be found when talking to the people of the *chō*.
In 1965 there was a tangible spirit of unity. There were problems, of course, but the area appears to have been an integral
part of the daily lives of the inhabitants. After dinner on hot
summer evenings while wives and daughters washed dishes, fathers
dressed in summer kimono would carry their children in piggyback
fashion as they strolled along the street greeting others, stop-
ping to peruse the latest weekly magazines at the stationery
store near the temple, or chatting with neighbors in the temple
courtyard as the children played with friends. Now there is almost none of that. Neighbors and neighborliness have taken on
restricted meaning. The feudal-era view of one's neighbors as
the families on the immediate right and left and the three families directly across the street (*mukō sangen ryō tonari*) may
still be prevalent, but no longer is there any broader feeling
that those people who live near the temple across the highway
have much in common with residents nearer Honda-machi. Indeed,
residents of one part of the old street center consistently refer to those on the other side of the highway as "people on the
other side" (*mukō no hitotachi*). This phrase implies more than
physical differentiation and separateness. The road has not
only made a dissection physically and politically in the neighborhood, but psychologically as well. Whether the *chōnaikai*
will succeed in mending the wound made by the sudden slicing of
the area into two is problematical. In 1972 Mr. Fuji was not
very optimistic.

Above, photo of Saiwai-chō neighborhood by day. Below, street scene of Saiwai-chō at night. Photos courtesy of Professor Richard A. Smith, School of Architecture and Allied Arts, University of Oregon at Eugene.

REPLACING THE CHŌNAIKAI:
POLITICAL AND ADMINISTRATIVE CHANGES

In April 1973, the city of Kanazawa established an Administrative Liaison Service System (*Gyōsei Renrakuin Seido*) to fulfill more effectively its many administrative responsibilities toward and to facilitate communication with its citizens. An Administrative Services Center (*Gyōsei Sābisu Shitsu*), located in the city hall and staffed by a few career officials of the city, is open to private citizens to hear suggestions, complaints, and to generally keep a dialogue going between the city and its residents. The Service Center appoints and supervises a team of paid liaison agents (*renrakuin*) who are distributed throughout the city on the basis of approximately one *renrakuin* per five-hundred households (Kanazawa Gikai Jimukyoku, 1976:99). These new administrative officials perform many of the same functions and services previously carried out by the unpaid, locally selected leaders of the *chōnaikai*. They maintain up-to-date family register records for their districts; distribute pamphlets, notices, and other information; collect family health insurance payments; accept and transmit requests and complaints from local residents regarding a host of matters in which the city has become involved; and represent the residents of their districts in meetings with officials of city departments. They are the municipal link with local neighborhoods and they are intended to foster a spirit of cooperation with the city. At times they are expected to meet with *chōnaikai* leaders in their districts to discuss matters relevant to the neighborhood. No longer are *chōnaikai* heads invited or encouraged to go directly to municipal offices to represent the *chō*. While they may do so as private citizens, they are seldom recognized as neighborhood leaders.

Kanazawa's reorganization of the city into liaison districts is being watched closely by other cities. Several teams of officials from some of Japan's largest cities have visited Kanazawa to investigate this system with the idea of implementing something like it in their cities. As the crush of urban expansion continues apace in Japan and the attendant problems of administration become more complex, bureaucracies are seeking means of dealing effectively with their increasing burdens and ways of maintaining communication with their constituents. A system such as that now used in Kanazawa where city hall can maintain control over the liaison agents is very enticing. From the standpoint of efficiency, Kanazawa's approach to the problem of urban administration and citizen-government communication is unique.

What has been the effect of this administrative change on the neighborhood? Mr. Fuji of the Hyakushinkai has indicated that since the *renrakuin* system went into effect, there is very little for the *chōnaikai* to do. In fact, they are left only with those activities associated with children's recreation and the fire watch. With the construction of ferroconcrete buildings and the development of modern fire departments the fire watcher making the rounds may also become a sight of bygone days. With Japan's new affluence, children's and youths' sporting activities such as baseball and volleyball teams have been supported by schools, companies, and other non-neighborhood agencies. From time to time a *chōnaikai* sponsors a boys baseball team, but the decline in *chōnaikai* funds bodes ill for this sort of continued involvement. Funds previously earmarked by the city for projects in the *chō* are no longer directly at the disposal of the *chōnaikai*, but are handled by the city government through its new *renrakuin* system. Residents who have begun to feel the futility of the *chōnaikai* as a viable organization have been lax in participating in activities that appear more like time-consuming chores than necessary and beneficial tasks.

Officials of the Service Center agree with local *chōnaikai* leaders that tasks previously reserved for the *chōnaikai* are now being undertaken by the *renrakuin*. But they argue that tasks are now being accomplished more efficiently inasmuch as the city can monitor the *renrakuin* and thereby bring its resources to bear more quickly in solving problems in the *chō*. The channeling of requests from the *renrakuin* to the Service Center where they are screened for significance, immediacy, and feasibility is pointed to as time- and money-saving; and this system is considered more equitable to all districts of the city when compared with the previous, informal system in which some *chōnaikai* heads asserted themselves at city hall while others were either too timid or put off requests until too late a date. Now, city administrators argue, everyone is treated alike. Moreover, since *renrakuin* are paid civil servants and come from the districts where they work, their activities can be directed toward achieving what is best for that district.

Chōnaikai leaders have argued that the city has become too involved in local neighborhood problems and that the *renrakuin* associate with the residents as officials from a higher authority. Despite the low posture that many of these *renrakuin* maintain in their relations with residents in their districts, they are still looked upon as representatives of the city. The idea of questioning city plans or making suggestions regarding the neighborhood through a city official is difficult for many Japanese. *Chōnaikai* leaders such as Mr. Fuji think it much easier for residents to

explain their views to a neighbor whom they have chosen to represent them rather than to one who has been appointed by the city
government. Political motives are attributed by the city to its
opposition in the words of one Service Center official, "Ideological bases are now being used by some of the *chōnaikai* to argue
against the liaison system and the fact of greater efficiency and
a better city for everyone_is being obscured" (personal interview,
Tokyo, June 1976). But *chōnaikai* leaders such as Mr. Fuji point
out that the sense of community is being lost and that it is not
being replaced by any comparable dedication to the larger entity
of the city through the new *renrakuin* system. Mr. Fuji believes
that active involvement in meaningful activities which benefit
one's family and neighbors is the key to neighborly solidarity
and draws people together. He is of the opinion that the city
in its effort to be efficient is doing too much for local inhabitants and instilling them with excessive expectations that government will or should do certain things for them. How far the city
will go in relieving neighborhoods of responsibilities is not
known, but the process to date appears to have had a debilitating
effect on neighborhood solidarity.

CONCLUSIONS

Saiwai-chō is a very small place in a very crowded land.
Some who hear that it is located in Kanazawa, a city with a repu-
tation for clinging to its feudal past, may dismiss the social
costs that have been exacted from its residents as merely an
overdue bill for having failed to change with the times. There
is no doubt that Kanazawa has begun to compete with other cities
to provide a better quality of life for its inhabitants. That
such honorable objectives should be pursued is not in question.
The problem arises when the benefits to be derived by the larger
entity of the nation, region, or city conflict with interests of
the smaller entity; in this particular case, the neighborhood.

In Saiwai-chō, the effects of the national and regional
plan to construct a highway and the city's program to restruc-
ture its administrative relationship with its citizens have both
had profound effects on the people living in the area. The ramifications of these changes go far beyond the physical changes
wrought in the *chō*, and will continue to impinge on the nature
of the local society. This is not to say that planners could
have foreseen the negative as well as the positive effects on
residents; but from what we have been able to ascertain, there
appears not to have been any effort to look much beyond the completion of the highway construction or the implementation of the
administrative liaison system. Often bureaucracies perceive the

world in terms of the need to carry out their charges efficiently and hence all too often they fail to realize that their solutions are accomplished at the expense of others. As long as it is easier to measure success by observing that a road has been built, that more pamphlets have been passed out, or more garbage collected in neighborhoods, the bureaucrats can continue to claim success in their work.

In the case of Saiwai-chō, one might argue that the void left in the previously closely knit neighborhood society occurred because of less than dynamic leadership, death or removal of local leaders, or the pressure of land on the value structures of people when land means money. Without doubt all of the above influenced the outcome in Saiwai-chō. But it may also be posited that even though the changes discussed in this paper were so overwhelming that Saiwai-chō could no longer return to what it previously had been, an investment of funds and efforts to reconstitute a proven system of neighborhood decision-making should have been made. While it is doubtful that a duplication of the active *chōnaikai* of pre-Mitsukuchi Plan days could have been brought about, or would even be desirable, the fact that the city chose to remove the decision-making process from the neighborhood by diluting the role of Saiwai-chō citizens caused those residents to become increasingly dependent on the city. Since the city is an echelon much further removed from the individual and the family than was the *chōnaikai*, the participatory role and the civic loyalties of Saiwai-chō residents may be diminished. Accordingly, these neighbors have become active Saiwai-chō residents less, but not Kanazawa citizens more.

Perhaps it should simply be said that Saiwai-chō is no different from any other place confronted by modern social transformation; that the loss of organizations of a former time is the toll required to travel the road to "modernity." The Japanese phrase, *"shikata ga nai"* (it can't be helped, or it's inevitable) perhaps best reflects the attitude of resignation so prevalent shortly after the Mitsukuchi project was completed in the Saiwai-chō area. In any event, this brief moment may become lost in history, one of those instances of "public and private adventures and crimes" in this neighborhood's motley progress toward modernization.

APPENDIX A

HYAKUSHINKAI KAIRANBAN

The following are the topics covered in the *kairanban* from about the first of April to late July, 1965.

1. Announcement of the general meeting of the *kodomokai*
   Announcement of the general meeting of the *chōnaikai*
   Notice of street repair to be begun soon
   Request for cooperation in making up the new *machi* name list
   Receipt of 1000 yen donation from Mr. U.

2. Report on the *kodomokai* meeting, and list of officers
   Kodomokai activities plan for the year
   Report on *funjinbu* trip to the Mt. Tenno area

3. List of the new *chōkai* officers
   List of the *hanchō*
   List of the *fujinbu*
   Notice of the rise in *chōkai* expenses due to repairs, etc.

4. April 28
   List of the *fujinbu* officers
   Recreation plans of the *fujinbu*
   Chōkai recreation plans
   List of dates on which the flag should be flown
   Information regarding cleaning of the *machi*

5. May 18
   Postponement of the *chōnaikai* trip to Noto
   Free use of the local school athletic grounds
   Local school representatives in the area
   Dates of *chōkai* assignments to direct traffic at school
       crossings
   Notice from the school regarding the use of playgrounds
   Reminder to keep the *machi* clean
   Traffic safety reminders

6. May 24
   Activities of the *kodomokai*
   Notice of the district volleyball tournament
   Announcement of *fujinbu* flower arrangement lessons
   Information regarding the use of insecticides
   Slogans for the summer (Get out for fresh air, Stay healthy,
       Eliminate traffic accidents)

(continued)

7. *May 29*
   Information regarding film and instructions on handling
       electrical appliances
   Information on the use of disinfectant
   Information about the Red Cross fund-raising campaign
   Report on a talk on city's urban renewal plans

8. *June 14*
   Announcement of team's victory in volleyball tournament
   Accouncement of roundtable discussion involving local teachers
   Plans for the trip to Mt. Tenno
   New arrivals in and departures from the machi

9. *June 21*
   Condolences for the death in the X household
   Information regarding the use of insecticides
   Information about participation in a fire insurance program
   Warning of accidents likely in the rainy season

10. *July 19*
    Plans for the trip to Mt. Tenno
    Notice about middle school students' collection of salable
        scrap
    Kodomokai machi-cleaning plans
    List of new families in the machi
    Effects of a small flood in the machi

11. *July 26*
    Schedule for the radio-led calisthenics
    Announcement of August recreational plans
    Information regarding visits to the machi by American uni-
        versity group

REFERENCES

Almond, Gabriel A., and James S. Coleman (Eds.), *The Politics of Developing Areas*. Princeton: Princeton University Press, 1960.

Black, Cyril E. *The Dynamics of Modernization: A Study in Comparative History*. New York: Harper and Row, 1966.

Hicks, Ursula. *The Large City: A World Problem*. New York: Macmillan Pub. Co., 1974.

Ishida, Takeshi, *Japanese Society*. New York: Random House, 1971.

Jansen, Marius B. (ed.) *Changing Japanese Attitudes Toward Modernization*. Princeton: Princeton University Press, 1965.

Kanazawashi Gikai Jimukyoku. *Kanazawa no Shisei* (Kanazawa Municipal Government). Kanazawa: Kanazawashi Gikai Jimukyoku, 1976.

Sansom, George B. *Japan: A Short Cultural History*. New York: Appleton-Century, 1962.

_____. *Japan in World History*. Tokyo, New York: International Secretariat, Institute of Pacific Relations, 1951.

Takeuchi, Keiichi. "The Rural Exodus in Japan--Basic Considerations for International Comparison." *Hitotsubashi Journal of Social Studies*, 7:1 (April, 1974); 8:1 (May, 1976).

In addition to the above material, I have relied heavily on numerous interviews of *chōnaikai* and city officials covering the period from 1965 to 1976.

GRF

Above, view of N. Okayama Tenmaya Department Store roof, December 1953. Below, same view, Summer 1964. Photos courtesy of Professor David H. Kornhauser, Department of Geography, University of Hawaii at Manoa.

IV

CITIZENS' MOVEMENTS IN URBAN AND RURAL JAPAN

*Margaret A. McKean**

INTRODUCTION

The phenomenon in Japan of citizens' movements, the majority of which are concerned with environmental and consumer problems, has received a great deal of attention recently.[1] Japan's rapid industrialization in the postwar era has caused pollution to spread almost unchecked, and has made Japan the world's leader in pollution diseases.[2] New to Japan, these citizens' movements are voluntary organizations composed primarily of ordinary citizens rather than simply of the usual intellectuals, students, labor leaders, and other members of the active political scene. They are issue-oriented, devoted to the political and social goals shared by their members, rather than to providing all-encompassing social fellowship. Members of these movements usually participate as individuals on the basis of their common objectives rather than through more diffuse traditional relationships. These movements would seem to be the sort of voluntary citizens' interest groups which are usually argued to be vital ingredients

*Margaret McKean is Assistant Professor of Political Science at Duke University, Durham, North Carolina. The dissertation research from which this article was drawn was supported in part by a William Harrison Mills Fellowship and a Dean's Fellowship from the University of California, Berkeley.

[1] The term residents' movements (jūmin undō) is usually used to identify all of these interest groups, and only the most politically sophisticated among them, whose members develop an awareness of their rights as individual citizens, are actually called citizens' movements (shimin undō).

[2] The numbers of pollution disease victims who receive relief payments under recent legislation are continually on the increase. By September 1975, there were 871 official victims (including 134 dead) of mercury poisoning in Kumamoto and Kagoshima Prefectures, 568 (including 28 dead) victims of mercury poisoning in Niigata Prefecture, 225 victims (including over 100 dead) of cadmium poisoning in Toyama Prefecture, 191 victims (including 24 dead) of hexavalent chromium poisoning, and over 2,700 mercury poisoning patients who are still awaiting final certification as victims. With the rapid increase in the number of areas designated as critical air pollution zones, there are now over 30,000 official air pollution victims. (See Japan Times, 12-14-74; 6-11-75; 7-6-75; 8-21-75; 8-27-75; and 9-3-75.

in a smoothly functioning democracy (Smith and Freedman, 1972).
In Japan, citizens' movements are thus widely hailed as manifestations of a developing democratic political culture.

An examination of the distribution and nature of citizens'
movements can tell us a great deal about changes in Japanese
political culture and about the social and political consequences
of rapid industrialization and urbanization in postwar Japan.
Citizens' movements have proliferated rapidly in Japan since 1970.
By conservative estimates there are now over 3,000 functioning
groups with about 1.5 million adults (see Appendix A). However,
they do not seem to be evenly distributed among urban and rural
areas. Opinion polls show that residents of the most urbanized
areas of Japan are about one and one-half times more likely than
the national average to feel uneasy and fearful about pollution
(Sorifu, 1972:7-8).

The greater tendency of urbanites to express antipollution
sentiment is more dramatic when we move from verbal responses in
opinion polls to indicators of concrete action. There are more
than twice as many formal pollution complaints per capita in the
highly urbanized prefectures as the national average (Kankyocho,
1972:312). We may conclude, then, that residents of highly urbanized areas are more likely to take concrete action in order
to protest against social ills than are those of the relatively
rural areas, who are also quite alarmed about pollution but not
so willing to express their grievances. This conclusion fits in
comfortably with what we know about the relatively greater
strength of traditional values in rural Japan--values which dis-
courage the open expression of conflict and emphasize community
harmony instead (Fukutake, 1967:155-222).

Perhaps the situation is not really so simple. Many of
the most well-known citizens' movements have arisen outside of
Japan's most urbanized and supposedly modern areas. Are these
exceptions to the rule, or is our picture of citizens' movements
distorted? Do citizens' movements build on a foundation of modern
democratic values as so many observers tell us, or can they also
utilize traditional values as a starting point? Are citizens'
movements in the most urban areas as individualistic and nontraditional as we expect, or is there variety even within this cate-
gory? If we find that many people can participate in these
movements on the basis of traditional values, can they maintain
these values unchanged, or will the experience of participating
in a political protest have some effect on their political attitudes? Is there any systematic variation in the choice of
protest methods adopted by these movements that might indicate
their interest in utilizing the resources available to citizens
in a democracy?

The literature available on well-known movements and my own work with activists from 14 movements in 8 prefectures provide a foundation for the answers to these questions, which will be presented below in detail. To collect the data used in this study, we used the available lists of citizens' movements and selected a sample of movements to include variation along most of the structural and behavioral dimensions which we found in the lists as a whole, and which warranted further examination and testing. Because it is impossible to locate or identify every existing citizens' movement, and also impossible to identify all the members of particular movements (there are no records), neither pure random sampling nor stratified sampling methods could be used. Instead, judgment sampling (see Ackoff, 1953:118-20) had to be relied upon, but great care was exercised to see that the sample of movements was as broadly representative as possible to permit reasonably safe generalizations of conclusions to the larger universe of citizens' movements as a whole.

The leaders of each of the 14 selected groups were contacted and arrangements made to interview group members. I personally interviewed each of the 64 respondents in the fall of 1972, conducting two- to three-hour interviews in Japanese. The interviews were coded and analyzed with nonparametric statistics suitable for use with small samples.

The data presented below will show that there is quite a wide variety of citizens' movements in Japan, and that there are significant distinctions among them in terms of (1) differences in the political and social circumstances in which they arise, (2) differences in the methods which they resort to, and (3) differences in the impact of the activist experience on the attitudes and beliefs of movement members.

THE ORIGINS OF PROTEST

MOTIVATION

First of all, even a cursory study of citizens' movements demonstrates that many of them have arisen in areas where traditional values are very strong. Further study of the values of individual participants shows that many rural environmental activists, and even some in highly urbanized areas, are initially motivated to join these movements for reasons other than an offended sense of individual political rights. First of all, pollution is so severe in some parts of Japan that antipollution citizens' movements can easily recruit many of their members by appealing to their survival instincts. In the present study we found that 31% of the activists were concerned about pollution primarily because they had already experienced its harmful effects, and that many had close relatives or friends who had suffered damage to their health. They were reluctant to vocalize their concern at first, due both to their own traditional belief that protest was inherently wrong and to pressure from others in the community to keep quiet. Finally, however, they would decide that the stakes were too high to remain silent. Concern over the consequences of pollution is often greater in semirural areas because most of Japan's fatal pollution diseases have occurred in nonurban areas, where water purification and sewage treatment are often inadequate or where new, massive industrial complexes have inundated areas with pollution.

A second source of motivation for prospective activists in these movements is their sense of community. To many activists, pollution is not only a personal threat to life and health, but it is also a threat to their community. They view their activism as a move made on behalf of their neighborhood or village. This is a particularly common source of motivation in rural areas facing the prospect of industrial development, but it also plays a part in mobilizing antipollution activists in some older urban communities. In the *shitamachi* (downtown) areas of Tōkyō, neighborhood associations have turned their attention to environmental problems because of this threat to change or even destroy their communities.[3]

The motivations we have mentioned so far can be significant in either rural or urban citizens' movements, although they are relatively common in rural areas. Rural movements have, in addition, a third argument which urban movements cannot use: that pollution is a by-product of industry that in and of itself is a threat to the agrarian way of life. A well-known movement in Kagoshima Prefecture, which has thus far prevented the construction of a massive petroleum refinery complex in Shibushi Bay, appeals to local residents' agrarian sentiments.[4] Movement

---

[3] Many observers would pointedly exclude these from a definition of citizens' movements or even residents' movement because they grow out of a previously existing organization. This one distinction aside, it is possible to argue that neighborhood associations have sometimes been a very important channel for the articulation of grievances in the formation of an effective antipollution movement, as discussed below.

[4] Unless indicated otherwise, the particular citizens' movements mentioned below are each described, and further references and documentation supplied, in Margaret A. McKean, "The Potential for Grass-Roots Democracy in Postwar Japan: The Anti-Pollution Movement as a Case Study in Political Activism" (unpublished Ph.D. dissertation, University of California, Berkeley, 1974), Chapter 5.

leaders argue that the proposed development in Shibushi is part of a general trend in Japan to industrialize at the expense of the agricultural population. They feel that industrialization goes hand in hand with the government's recent attempts (1) to lower the fixed rice price, (2) to do away with payments for leaving paddy land uncultivated, (3) to decrease tariffs on imports of foreign agricultural goods, (4) to import more food from abroad in order to reduce Japan's balance of trade surplus, and (5) to tax agricultural land so heavily that farming becomes impossible.

Shibushi Bay movement leaders argue that in the past Japan's agricultural population has been forced to subsidize industrialization by shouldering a heavy tax burden and by accepting a lower standard of living than city dwellers. They feel that government and industry now plan to deliver the final blow: to force farmers to abandon their tranquil, simple, pleasant way of life by bringing industry to their doorstep. Thus, in their view, opposition to one particular petrochemical *kombinat* becomes part of a more general strategy to obtain an adequate standard of living for farmers by revitalizing agriculture so that farmers do not have to turn to other occupations, and to defend Japan's agricultural sector against what they regard as the malicious scheming of industrialists who now control the government and the ruling party. The Shibushi movement is particularly interesting because it has adopted many modern forms and methods in order to express hostility toward modern industrial society and to defend traditional agrarian values.

In contrast to these traditional or nonpolitical motivations, some movements in highly urbanized areas have used sophisticated arguments based on citizens' political rights. Two well-known protests arose in upper middle-class residential areas of western Tōkyō to oppose metropolitan construction projects. The citizens claimed to have the right to be consulted and to influence final decisions regarding such projects. Residents of Takaido in Suginami ward opposed the construction of a sanitation plant in the area, and residents in Nerima and Toshima wards have resisted the construction of a proposed highway. In both of the above cases the proposed construction threatened what could be called a local "sense of community," but movement activists did not fear the destruction of the social bonds in a traditional collectivity so much as they feared destruction of the attractiveness of their residential area and the resulting decline in land values. Both movements complained that the metropolitan government finalized the plans without ever consulting the citizens who would be affected and without inviting their complaints or suggestions. Individual activists in both

of these movements often referred to their fundamental belief
that they had a right to influence the decisions made by their
local government.

It is significant that these movements were in upper middle-
class areas where most residents were well-educated, attentive to
current affairs, and relatively demanding about the standard of
performance they expected from government. The importance of
this "modern" political orientation as a factor in the mobilization of these movements becomes clearer by comparison with antipollution protests in the *shitamachi* areas of Tōkyō, where the
focus is on community, neighborhood, and a traditional sense of
fairness based on mutual obligations, and where there is no mention of citizens' rights at all.

LEADERSHIP AND GROUP STRUCTURE

The values and motivations of an antipollution citizens'
movement are closely related to the type of leadership and the
group structure that emerge. Generally speaking, the more traditional the motivations and values of the members themselves,
the more likely the movement is to have a leader who is a well-
respected member of the community. The more traditional the
motives of participants, the more likely that the leader will
have to assume the role and functions of the traditional parent
figure in a paternalistic patron-client relationship by elicit-
ing the active contributions of the members' time and energy
in the form of personal obligations they owe to him. The presence of a figure of this sort can be essential not only during
recruitment but also later when the movement usually experiences
bitter conflict with the rest of the community.

If both the community as a whole and the antipollution
movement members are bound up in the network of personal relationships which form the geographical core of support organizations for conservative politicians, the movement leadership
plays a critical role in legitimizing the act of protest. In
Shibushi, for instance, leaders of the antipollution movement
were Liberal Democratic Party (LDP) notables (doctors, lawyers,
priests, and maverick local politicians) who had regularly delivered votes to two Diet members in the national LDP leadership
who favored industrial development in Shibushi. Because these
local antipollution leaders decided to pursue their antipollution
objective to its logical political conclusion, they advocated
that voters support Socialist (JSP) or Communist (JCP) candidates
in the December 1972 elections rather than the LDP. The example
set by such leaders, in a movement whose members were reluctant

to oppose the conservative LDP establishment, was probably essential in stimulating antipollution activists to change old habits and reconsider long-held beliefs.

In contrast to these movements in rural areas (and, I might add, in *shitamachi* areas of Tōkyō), which depend so much on the initiatives and precedents set by their leaders, the more politicized movements of middle-class urban areas find the whole idea of leadership quite unimportant. Where the motivations of individual activists are strong and where their commitment to protest and opposition in the context of the environmental issue is unafflicted by cross-pressures, activists do not need leaders who set examples, or exhort them to action, or legitimize protest. They need only a small clerical staff at most.

Urban activists are more likely to have prior experience in social protest and to have sympathies with local opposition parties--so they are not as timid or apprehensive as rural activists about the act of protest itself. They are more accustomed than rural activists to evaluating issues on their merits and to act, vote, and protest if necessary. Their higher education and exposure to a variety of political belief systems, including postwar democratic concepts, gives them this freedom of action.

An important aspect of movement structure is the role played by existing neighborhood associations, which varies within both urban and rural areas according to the impact of the particular pollution issue. If the association leaders themselves feel threatened by local pollution, if antipollution sentiment accumulates rapidly, and if the vast majority of residents in the neighborhood are concerned, local leaders may very well take up the antipollution cause themselves and function as organizers and spokesmen for the movement. Such was the case in Tōkyō's garbage war in both Suginami ward (Takaido) and Koto (Edagawa district), where sentiment in the most seriously afflicted neighborhoods was strong and volatile and where neighborhood association leaders shared a sense of personal vulnerability with other neighborhood residents. This was also the case in the city of Mishima in 1964, where 80-90% of the city's entire population rapidly coalesced around an antipollution stance, and where those who owned the land which petroleum companies wanted to buy agreed unanimously not to sell (see Matsubara, 1971:213).

When the conflict between the antipollution movement and local levels of government is quite bitter, neighborhood association leaders usually have to choose sides. They feel

cross-pressure, torn between their two traditional roles as channels of administration from the top down on important matters and
as transmitters of community views upward on lesser matters. Often,
neighborhood leaders do not particularly sympathize with the local antipollution movement or cannot bring themselves to break
the strong social and personal ties that link them to upper layers
of the administrative structure. In such cases, local concern
over pollution or development may dissolve for lack of leadership
and cohesion, as in Falconeri's Saiwai-cho. If sentiment is
stronger, a citizens' movement will form outside of the frame-
work of existing neighborhood organizations to fight city hall
on its own terms.[5]

A final source of variation to be mentioned concerns the
differences in internal group structure. The traditional sorts
of groups more common in rural areas have a hierarchical structure, prefer to arrive at unanimous decisions through consensual
politics, argue that unity and cohesion are more important to
success than the size of the movement, and develop a strong
we-they consciousness which creates a reluctance to accept help
from anyone who is not a community member sharing the same problems. They hold the traditional belief that unity of spirit and
depth of conviction enable people to overcome otherwise insuper-
able odds.

An extreme contrast with this kind of internal structure
is provided by the urban movement which opposed highway construction through Nerima ward in Tōkyō. In that group, the absence
of a firm boundary between members and nonmembers made it impossible for them to develop a hierarchical structure or any we-they
consciousness. Help from outside the neighborhood was welcomed,
and decisions were made by a majority vote of those who attended
formal meetings rather than by consensus. In contrast to the
rural activists, those in Nerima claimed that the size of a
movement had a great deal to do with its effectiveness.

LOCAL POLITICAL ENVIRONMENT

In part, the relatively traditional character of rural
movements in comparison to the willingness of urban antipollution
activists to modify traditional modes of group behavior is a

---

[5]This was the case in an interesting group not included within the survey, in a
lower-class Tōkyō neighborhood where local housewives concerned about a variety of traffic
and pollution problems could not persuade their very stodgy neighborhood association leadership to take up these issues. The women formed their own citizens' group as a result
and are now considered to be a "shadow" neighborhood association, the appropriate body to
turn to if one is concerned with local politics or social problems rather than with
drinking or festivals.

matter of "lag" created by the process of urbanization itself.
But there is also a pragmatic dimension to the preference of
rural activists for traditional procedures. Traditional practices provide the psychological comfort and the organizational
strength needed by rural antipollution movements because they
face tremendous hostility from the surrounding community and
from local government. Rural movements need firm leadership,
strong organization, and continuous reinforcement of members'
cohesion around the common goal. Precisely because protest is
not considered acceptable in most nonurbanized areas, activists
in citizens' movements in these areas need constant bolstering
in order to justify their behavior to themselves and in order
to withstand the kinds of pressure they experience from non-
activist friends and relatives, and from business associates
who threaten to use economic sanctions against them. Sometimes
farmers and fishermen involved in citizens' movements are de-
prived of essential services by their local cooperative, and
rural activists may be socially and economically ostracized by
the rest of their community.

Industrial development in rural areas is a divisive and
controversial issue. The very poor in such a community are
usually willing to abandon traditional livelihoods in order to
increase their standard of living. Even among those who have
no significant material motive to advocate industrial development, many are traditional enough in orientation to feel that
it is indecent, immoral, and "egoistic" to assert one's opinions
and objections to any program presented by local authorities.
In contrast to this, urban citizens' movements often deal with
problems which do not divide the community into hostile factions.
Environmental issues in urban areas are more complex, and those
who would benefit from ignoring them are not concentrated in
any identifiable pocket of the community. Urban citizens' movements face a hostile community less often than they face an
indifferent one. Furthermore, the social and political atmos-
phere in urbanized areas is more supportive of dissent and opposition, which are no longer regarded as immoral.

It is not only the local community which hinders antipollution movements in rural areas. They also face hostile
local governments. Until the late 1960s, both conservatives
and leftists in Japan favored the goals of industrialization
and economic growth. Thus, local governments in rural areas
have regarded industrial development projects as very desirable,
and politicians have built their careers by promising to bring
development. With the rise of citizens' movements to oppose
haphazard industrial growth, local politicians, upset and very
often utterly bewildered by opposition from what they view as

irresponsible troublemakers trying to interfere, have sometimes resorted to illegal measures to circumvent these objections.

Activists in Ōiso, who tried unsuccessfully to oppose the construction of a chemical plant, reported that the local mayor and the plant owners cooperated in efforts to buy up the necessary land secretly and to bribe some local residents to disrupt the opposition movement. When the plant started production anyway in September 1972, the movement went to court charging the mayor and the company with illegal procedures. In Usuki, where a citizens' movement to prevent construction of a cement factory acted more quickly, the local mayor's illegal promises to the factory owners and other unseemly deeds were exposed early, and the movement succeeded in its efforts, winning favorable verdicts in District and Higher Courts in July 1971 and October 1972.[6]

Urban antipollution activists, however, encounter more sympathetic, flexible local governments which usually compromise without resorting to extreme measures to protect their original proposals. Urban local governments operate in a complex environment where they have long experience at compromising their plans due to objections from many sources. But what would appear to make the most significant difference in the behavior of local governments is that many of the urban mayors and governors are reformist, strongly committed to democratic procedures and to the role of local government as a channel of citizen influence rather than as an administrative arm of the national government. Even though citizens' movements in urban areas may be disappointed with the inadequate response of reformist local governments to their plight, they usually do not have to contend with the same indifference to formal legal procedures and the same neglect of citizen opinion as do movements in rural areas.

GOALS: POLLUTION PREVENTION *VS.* COMPENSATION

A final circumstantial factor affecting the nature of citizens' movements is whether the central goal is to prevent future pollution or to obtain compensation for pollution damage already done. Activists in a movement intending to prevent pollution

---

[6]Information about the legal procedures being contested in lawsuits in Ōiso is not available in a published source, but all of the informants in the sample (including one of the mayor's former best friends) raised this issue independently, without any probing on the interviewer's part. The movements in both Ōiso and Usuki are more fully described in McKean, 1974, but the reader may also note that there are references available on Usuki which do discuss the illegal activities of local politicians and local government. See Matsushita Ryūichi, <u>Kanashi no Onnatachi: Aru Gyoson no Tatakai</u> (The Women of Kazanashi: The Struggle of a Fishing Village) (Tōkyō: Asahi Shimbunsha, 1972, passim).

have to think about desirable alternative policies, therefore
about policy-making, and hence about citizen participation in
decisions. Activists in a movement aiming only at compensation
need not move away from a traditional concept of fairness in order
to justify their involvement: that the suffering and downtrodden
deserve some recompense.

Both prevention- and compensation-oriented movements occur
in urban and rural settings. In the urban areas where most antipollution activists are already well-educated and informed citizens aware that they have political rights, participation in
prevention-oriented movements simply strengthens these democratic
political attitudes and beliefs. But in rural areas, where re-
cruits to prevention-oriented antipollution movements lack this
awareness, participation increases their familiarity with citizens' rights and the available methods for exerting influence on
government.

THE EVOLUTION OF TACTICS

Antipollution movements use a wide variety of methods.
Matsubara Haruo describes the evolution from *petition-style movement* (typified by the earliest stages in almost all movements but
rapidly abandoned by more sophisticated groups), to the *direct
action* or *explosion movement* (this is likely to happen to a
petition movement when it learns that petitions have no impact),
to the full-fledged *citizens' movement* which uses a full battery
of modern techniques (Matsubara, 1971:183-242; Tsuru, 1968:256-
59). Some individual movements pass through this entire evolution of methods themselves, but many newly arisen movements
profit from the experience of their predecessors by passing
rapidly into the "citizen" stage. Thus, this pattern of linear
evolution corresponds to increasing sophistication over time
within any individual movement and among citizens' movements as
a whole. It also helps us to distinguish between rural movements
which devote a great deal of time to traditional techniques such
as petitions and urban movements which quickly resort to newer
methods.

PETITIONS

Most movements pass through the same stages of development.
As White's findings would lead us to expect, concerned residents
voice their complaints first through the most familiar institu-
tional channels--local neighborhood associations. They submit
petitions, phrased as humble requests toward the *okami* (superiors)
rather than as forthright demands based on any awareness of

citizens' rights. These organizations are usually led by *yuryo-
kusha* (powerful people), who are almost always conservative in
affiliation, and whose influence is in part based on their association with the same local politicians and industrialists who
are the targets of the complaints.

Because of preexisting personal ties, neighborhood association leaders may not do a very good job of transmitting the in-
tensity, anger, fear, or concern about pollution that lies behind
the petitions and complaints of neighborhood residents.[7] These
leaders may readily accept mild reassurances and weak compromises,
and according to some sources they are very easily "bought off"
by the vested interests which seek either to protect the polluting
industry or to promote a highly polluting regional development
plan.[8] This process of "buying off" is not necessarily sinister,
and indeed many neighborhood leaders may sincerely believe that
they have performed their function to the fullest by being taken to
dinner at a teahouse at the expense of industry executives and
telling them, over much beer and rice wine, how worried the community is. As far as they are concerned, this is the normal
Japanese political process and the one which produces the best
results. Thus the vertical personal ties between neighborhood
leaders and conservative politicians at the municipal and prefectural levels may serve to further soften and moderate the tone
of already humble petitions (Matsubara, 1971:187).

Local residents may not immediately be dissatisfied with
these responses and may persist for months or even years at
submitting petitions through their neighborhood leaders. However,
it is generally agreed that no movement has achieved its objectives by relying only on petitions.[9] If repeated frustration is
encountered at the neighborhood association level, some movements

---

[7]It is significant that respondents in this study volunteered this explanation for
their frequent discouragement with neighborhood associations.

[8]See Jūmin ni Yori Keiji Baipasu Kōgai Kenkyū Gurūpu (Residents' Pollution Research
Group on the Kyōtō-Shiga Bypass), Kōgai Yosoku to Taisaku (Pollution: Forecasts and Counter-
measures) (Tōkyō: Asahi Shimbunsha, 1971), p. 251; Matsubara Haruo, Kōgai to Chiiki Shakai:
Seikatsu to Jūmin Undō no Shakaigaku (Pollution and Regional Society: The Sociology of
Livelihood and Residents' Movements) (Tōkyō: Nihon Keizai Shimbunsha, 1971), pp. 179-91;
Shoji Hikaru and Miyamoto Ken'ichi, Osorubeki Kōgai (Fearful Pollution) (Tōkyō: Iwanami
shoten, 1964), pp. 194-96; and Tsuru Shigeto, Gendai Shihonshugi to Kōgai (Modern Capitalism
and Pollution) (Tōkyō: Iwanami shoten, 1968), pp. 271-86.

[9]See for example, Matsubara pp. 183-242; Miyamoto Ken'ichi, "Jūmin Undō no Riron to
Rekishi" (The Theory and History of Residents' Movements), in Miyamoto Ken'ichi and Endō
Akira, eds. Toshi Mondai to Jūmin Undō (Urban Problems and Residents' Movements), Volume 8:
Gendai Nihon no Toshi Mondai (Urban Problems in Modern Japan) (Kyōtō: Sekibunsha, 1971),
p. 64; Ui Jun, Kōgai no Seijigaku: Minamata Byō wo Megutte (The Politics of Pollution: On
Minamata Disease) (Tōkyō: Sanseidō, 1968), p. 197; and Ui Jun, Kōgai Genron (A Discussion
on Pollution), Volume III (Tōkyō: Aki shobo, 1971), p. 217-219.

may fade.[10] Others, however, decide to mobilize on their own to create new independent organizational channels for pooling their efforts and exploring new tactics.

DIRECT ACTION

In the earliest days of antipollution movements, the climate for this unusual form of activism--circumventing (or transforming) neighborhood associations and traditional petitioning techniques by creating alternative voluntary associations and by using other methods--was not very favorable, and few helpful precedents existed as guides. Some movements were disappointed with the failure of petitions, but were also uninformed and inexperienced about alternatives. Their anger and fear unabated, their energy sometimes exploded in the form of direct action. For example, activists might blockade plants to force them to cease operations, fill effluent pipes with concrete, or even invade the premises and destroy machinery. Sometimes direct action is used as an emergency measure to bargain for time until lawsuits can be filed, court injunctions delivered, or negotiations recommenced.

Most environmental activists regard direct action as an unwise technique, largely because it alienates public opinion and relies on tactics which come close to violating the law. One result of direct action is usually negotiation or formal arbitration between the movement and the offending company. However, lacking bargaining skills and not always willing to resort to other methods, many of the early movements did not win very favorable settlements by this means. Over time, antipollution movements began to experiment with less conventional methods of exerting influence.[11]

---

[10] As we have seen, neighborhood association leaders are also capable of changing their own political orientation and converting their organizations into vehicles for the antipollution cause, rather than being co-opted by the administrative structure above them. Thus traditional neighborhood associations can function as interest articulation structures, as James White describes in Paper V, if their leaders choose to allow this.

[11] Now that politicians and industrialists realize that movements are willing to use the politically sophisticated methods described later in this paper, they are much more willing to make concessions early in a controversy. Thus, today's movements are able to take advantage of the travails of their predecessors and can quickly extract rather favorable settlements from negotiation and arbitration processes. All of the major court cases have been followed by renegotiated settlements on behalf of the victims who did not file suit, and it is now customary for damage payments to include automatic cost of living increases. For a discussion of the effectiveness of citizens' movements which resort to direct action today, see "Peasant Uprisings and Citizens' Revolts," in Japan Interpreter 3:3 (Autumn, 1973), pp. 279-83. For a discussion of the trend for financial compensation to increase over time, see McKean, Chapter 2.

LEGAL AND POLITICAL METHODS

One new technique is the *single-share movement*, used when
the target of an antipollution movement is one particular enter-
prise. Activists and their sympathizers purchase single shares
in the offending company and, for what is a very low admission
fee, thus acquire full participation rights in shareholders'
meetings. This is often the only way they ever manage to confront
a company's senior officials in person (Gotō, 1971; Ui, 1971a:163-
77, 1971b:51-54). Participation in shareholders' meetings has a
number of advantages. First, by using this forum to present
their complaints and in some cases to describe their suffering,
activists put company management into the inescapable position
of having to admit personal responsibility if they uphold traditional values. On the other hand, even if company management
no longer responds in terms of traditional obligations and attempts instead to suppress participation by the single-share
owners, the activists in the antipollution movement win a great
deal of favorable publicity.

This method has also proven to have legal value.[12] Dissi-
dent shareholders who are denied their right to speak at meetings
can file lawsuits. A verdict handed down in March 1974 declared
all the resolutions made at a particular meeting of a major polluting company (Chisso, the offender in the Minamata mercury poisoning) to be null and void on these grounds (*Japan Times*, March 29,
1974).[13] However, through this act of filing a lawsuit, an
antipollution movement enters the "citizen" stage--as litigation
is not part of the traditional repertoire of protest.

It is not until the citizen stage that antipollution movements have their best chances for success. They employ a wide
variety of modern political tactics, including participation in
election campaigns to remove from office public officials who
fail to reflect their wishes. This change involves a very important re-definition of roles on the part of antipollution activists. No longer do they refer their problems to paternalistic
benefactors and overseers who carry a diffuse responsibility to
take care of all problems--personal and political. Rather, the
citizens' movements realize that what control they have over the

---

[12]It is also a source of great pleasure to these owners of single shares that their
meager contribution of a few yen to the company treasury costs the company from 5 to 10
times that amount annually to cover clerical costs because of legal obligations to mail
invitations to meetings, ballots, and announcements of decisions to all shareholders.

[13]Firms often control the meetings by hiring sōkaiya, a specialized variety of gangster. Since the verdict against Chisso, the National Police Agency has begun to crack
down on gangster organizations which indulge in this practice and on company officials who
hire them.

industry in question is legal and political: the power to file suit, to approve or deny construction permits, to supply or with-hold municipal facilities, to enforce environmental standards, and so forth. Thus they learn that they can best approach the problem through the courts and local government. *Activists whose movements reach the citizen stage no longer define themselves as anonymous victims, but as citizens who have rights which must be asserted and protected.*

Rural and urban citizens' movements differ in the techniques that they find useful at this stage. Rural movements are much more likely to be involved in disputes that lend themselves to resolution in the courts, because there are violations of law and conspicuous offenders present. Urban movements do not often face such clear-cut situations so they must rely on interest group tactics and lobbying. Similarly, rural movements can make better use of local elections because there is greater congruence be-tween boundaries of election districts and boundaries of areas afflicted by pollution problems (usually the entire village or town).

It would appear that since urban movements have only inter-mediate devices at their disposal, they should have more diffi-culty achieving success. We have seen, however, that urban citi-zens' movements usually operate in a more sympathetic environ-ment and need not resort to such powerful methods in order to make their point. Tireless publicity efforts, lobbying through local representatives, and negotiating with municipal metropoli-tan officials involved in city planning or environmental protec-tion are usually sufficient.

Urban movements deal with politicians and officials who are not so likely to be involved in the sort of social infra-structure that supports the conservative party in smaller towns and rural areas. The process of urbanization is rapidly doing away with these traditional political forms. Thus, politicians and officials in areas which are already highly urbanized and industrially developed do not have strong personal motives to preserve the *status quo,* to enact a proposed construction project without amendment, or to defer to the wishes of local industri-alists (in large urban areas there are too many diverse inter-ests to produce a united front), and thus they are freer to ac-commodate citizen requests. Activists in urban citizens' move-ments spend less time searching for ways to get attention and to exert pressure, and more time studying the particular pollu-tion problem at hand and participating personally in the process of designing alternative urban plans and draft legislation. Rural citizens' movements face primarily political obstacles, whereas

urban movements usually manage to overcome these and go on to a
consideration of the physical and financial limitations govern-
ing the solutions.

Thus it takes the rural activists who have usually participated in election campaigns in the context of their movement.
They often uncover transgressions of political ethics and sometimes violations of law, and hence they gradually reach the
painful conclusion that they cannot trust their social superiors
to protect their interests, but must undertake that responsibility
themselves. Where antipollution movements have entered the electoral arena, they have frequently campaigned successfully on behalf of antipollution candidates for municipal and prefectural
assemblies and have managed to elect sympathetic mayors in many
cities.

Very large antipollution movements have launched recall
campaigns against "pro-pollution" mayors and assemblymen. Although recall is explicitly mentioned in the 1947 constitution,
it is an unfamiliar notion to Japanese and they are reluctant
to engage in this sort of blatantly open conflict. Recall attempts built around the pollution issue have failed more often
than they have succeeded, and the results have often been ambiguous. The village of Rokkasho in Aomori Prefecture was deep-
ly divided over the issue of industrial development, and both
sides of the controversy attempted to use recall to oust local
officials who favored their respective opponents. Although the
votes in both elections were close, both officials survived recall and were honorably reinstated, which might indicate that
voters in this conservative community were more hostile to the
idea of recall than to pollution or to industrial development
(*Japan Times*, Jan. 10, May 15, and June 5, 1973). In Usuki,
the antipollution citizens' movement waged a very powerful campaign to recall the mayor for his involvement in inviting a company to build a cement plant there; not only did they quickly
exceed the minimum necessary number of signatures on their recall
petition, they actually collected signatures from a majority of
the city's eligible voters. The mayor resigned in fear, and one
month later the city held a mayoral replacement election in
December 1970 instead of the intended recall. However, the recently resigned mayor recouped enough strength to win reinstate-
ment by a small margin for the remainder of his term. Nonetheless, he did not try to run for another term, and an antipollution candidate was victorious in the next regular mayorality
election (*Japan Times*, December 14, 1970; see also Matsushita,
1972:158-87).

What is significant here is that citizens' movements have explored their political resources. Even a recall attempt that fails can come close enough to succeeding so that the offending official decides not to run for reelection (as in Usuki), and the same objectives are achieved. Similarly, even when a movement elects fewer antipollution candidates than it had hoped, the winners are sufficiently nervous about their own political careers to pay attention to the demands of the local antipollution movement. This is also one reason why urban citizens' movements can lobby effectively with local governments without resorting to recall campaigns or participating in elections: urban politicians have already learned from the steady increase in reformist representation at the local level that their constituents are capable of voting them out of office. In rural areas where voters have not previously exhibited such careful attention to the issues, politicians assume themselves to be relatively invulnerable and thus force citizens' movements to the ultimate test of electoral competition.

Even where citizens' movements remain small, their entrance into the electoral arena may function to sharpen political awareness in the rest of the community; such areas often experience an increase in reformist assemblymen and mayors some time later, after the demise of the citizens' movement. Where citizens' movements have been created because neighborhood associations failed to transmit effectively the wishes of their members to municipal authorities, the leaders of these associations, along with local assemblymen and mayors, have been known to reverse their positions completely. Conservative politicians who join the antipollution bandwagon do so not as a temporary gesture to appease a small group of dissidents, but in recognition of the fact that the local citizens' antipollution movement has come to represent the sentiments of the overwhelming majority of the community. Their political survival now depends upon their ability to stand firm as representatives of those citizens *vis à vis* industry and higher levels of government.

THE IMPACT OF ACTIVISM ON INDIVIDUALS

Thus far we have discussed citizens' movements as organic wholes, but a complete analysis of the values and beliefs which they represent requires us to examine individual activists within the movements. Although we have argued that the most effective movements are those which advance to the "citizen stage" in that they learn to use the full range of political tools at their disposal, we have not yet established whether this same progression takes place in individual members. As we will show below, there

was considerable variety in the nature of the activist experience
and in the extent to which individuals changed attitudes and beliefs on the basis of their participation.

THE PAROCHIAL ACTIVIST

Activists in urban and rural[14] movements come from very
different backgrounds, join their respective movements with very
different expectations and attitudes, and undergo different experiences as activists. In this study these rural counterparts
were relatively less educated, less experienced at social protest,
interested in narrow objectives and very specific pollution problems, and motivated to activism out of immediate self-interest
rather than altruism. The urban activists were better educated,
likely to be veterans of protest, concerned about broad objectives and larger environmental issues, and more motivated by
general concern than by immediate fear for their own well-being.

A "sophistication" index was created from the variables
representing these tightly interrelated dimensions.[15] As Table 1
shows, there was a close association between sophistication and
urban residence. Seventy percent of the cases in the sample fell
into two clusters which we call "rural isolates" and "urban
sophisticates." Each cluster represents a different "ideal
type" of activist and a different way of approaching environmental
activism. However, it should be pointed out that there existed
in addition to these two ideal types a smaller, third cluster of
cases, "urban isolates." Analysis of each of these individuals
indicates that by and large they are respondents from *shitamachi*
areas or those of relatively low socioeconomic status.

One of the most important points to be made about these
findings is that only 41% of the respondents based their activism on sophisticated motives and concerns. Indeed, there may
exist sampling bias which would require us to assume that in the
universe of all citizens' movements, such sophisticated activists

---

[14]Rural activists are defined as those residing in towns under 30,000 in size or
those whose occupation was farming or fishing. Urban activists are those living in cities
of over 40,000 population (but almost all of the urban respondents in this survey live in
very large cities of the Greater Tōkyō area).

[15]A "sophistication" index was generated from the six variables representing these
tightly interrelated dimensions by selecting them from a large trial correlation matrix,
trichotomizing the responses, scoring them uniformly (with values of -1, 0, or 1) so
that the correlation coefficients in the remaining six rows and columns of the correlation matrix all became positive, and adding the scores (for a description of the items
used, see Appendix B). The index acquired its name simply from the fact that several of
the constituent variables seemed to be related to levels of cognitive complexity and
imagination.

are far fewer than this 41%. In rural Japan, where some of the
largest and most effective movements are located, one is extremely unlikely to encounter "sophisticated" activists at all.
The urban and rural isolates together, then, form a majority of
activists who engage in political protest because of narrowly
conceived, localized concerns, rather than the elegant and noble
motives that we might have expected to find among environmentalists. These findings have two rather important implications.
First, these "isolated" activists are presumably unlikely to ap-
ply their concern with pollution to problems outside the com-
munity--so there are obvious limitations on the possibility of
creating any kind of coalition of environmentalists which would
be able to lobby effectively at the national level. But on the
other hand, we must admit that a parochial vision is certainly
no impediment to political activism at the local level. Indeed,
it is possible to conclude that the intense local concerns which
motivate parochial activists can enhance the political influence
of ordinary citizens in traditional communities and can make
local authorities responsive to a wider range of local needs.

THE DISILLUSIONED SWITCHER

We have established that urban and rural activists differ
from each other in background characteristics and in the levels
of sophistication with which they approach political protest.
It is also possible to argue that the activist experience itself has a differential impact on members of rural and urban
movements. This is probably shown most clearly by changes in
the political parties which activists support and by attitudes
toward the political spectrum in general. The activists in this
study were predominantly (58%) reformist (supportive of the
Japan Socialist [JSP] and Japan Communist [JCP] parties) even
before joining antipollution movements, so they clearly leaned
more toward the left than the general population did. However,
it is clear from Table 2 that participation in citizens' movements had a pronounced effect upon conservative recruits--nearly
half of whom switched to support of the left as a result of
their activist experience.[16] Significantly, this effect was
considerably greater in rural areas in that rural activists
who joined their movements as conservatives were twice as
likely as urban activists to abandon the Liberal Democrats in
favor of the left. Furthermore, no one switched in the op-
posite direction, not even among leftists unhappy with an inadequate response from reformist local governments.

---

[16] It should be noted that respondents were asked at a different point in the interview about their actual voting habits, and that switchers did change their votes
as well as their attitudes.

TABLE 1

ISOLATION AND SOPHISTICATION AMONG RURAL AND URBAN ANTIPOLLUTION ACTIVISTS

Isolation-Sophistication Index

	Isolation								Sophistication					
	-6	-5	-4	-3	-2	-1	0	1	2	3	4	5	6	
Rural	13	8	21	8	17	17	13	0	4	0	0	0	0	101%
Urban	0	0	3	10	8	13	4	4	13	18	18	4	4	99%

$$Tau\ b = .544^*$$
$$p = .001$$
$$N = 64$$

Scatterplot

Urban Isolates (N=13)   Urban   Urban Sophisticates (N=25)

Rural Isolates (N=20)   Rural   Rural Sophisticates (N=1)

See note to Table 1 on top of following page.

**Because Tau b takes ties into account, it is simultaneous-
ly a more sensitive, yet also more conservative, measure than
Tau c, which is occasionally recommended for rectangular tables
in preference to Tau b (see Norman Nie et al., Statistical Package for the Social Sciences, Second Edition [New York: McGraw-
Hill, 1975], p. 277).*

*In addition, p values (levels of significance for the N
used in calculating Tau b) have also been presented with the
tables. In fact, it is not actually legitimate to engage in
statistical inference or perform tests of significance with this
data, because strict probability sampling could not be used.*

TABLE 2

CHANGES IN PARTICIPATION AMONG RURAL AND
URBAN ANTIPOLLUTION ACTIVISTS

Item	Rural	Urban	Total
AMONG ANTIPOLLUTION ACTIVISTS			
Conservative Standpatters	17%	25%	22%
Disillusioned Switchers*	29	15	20
Reformist Standpatters	54	60	58
Total	100%	100%	100%
			$(N = 64)$
AMONG FORMER CONSERVATIVES ONLY			
Conservative Standpatters	36%	63%	52%
Disillusioned Switchers*	64	38	48
Total	100%	101%	100%

$(N = 27)$
$Tau\ b = .313**$
$p = .025$

**Disillusioned Switchers consist only of those who switched
partisanship from the conservative to reformist parties. No respondent switched in the other direction.
**See note to Table 1 at the top of this page.*

If we examine changes in partisanship along with several comprehensive indices of attitudes toward reference objects from left to the right of the political spectrum (see Tables 3-5), we can see the differential effects of antipollution activism.[17]

First of all, we see in Table 3 that rural and urban activists were surprisingly alike in their intensely negative attitudes toward conservative symbols--the urbanites largely because of their partisan predispositions, and rural activists because of the intensely bitter experience they had with conservative local administrations. The fact that rural activists gave negative ratings to local mayors and governors (who were usually conservative) while urban activists gave positive ratings to their heads of local government (who were often reformist) verifies our conclusion that activists based much of their attitude on the behavior of politicians at the local level. However, urban activists were not particularly favorable toward the political left either, whereas rural activists were quite pleased with leftist politicians who offered their time, support, advice, and political experience. As a result of the relatively greater positive feeling toward the left, then, rural activists were considerably less cynical or hostile than the urbanites toward politics as a whole.

Urban activists were disappointed relative to their expectations of aid from the JSP (Socialist) or JCP (Communist). In urban areas where the leftist parties were in power, the JSP and JCP were often in the embarrassing position of officially campaigning on behalf of antipollution movements while quietly discouraging specific movements which might discredit local leftist administrations in power. Nonetheless, even though urban activists were sometimes disillusioned by the half-hearted, equivocal cooperation they received, they recognized both the precarious position of the left and the physical limitations involved in trying to balance their demands along with many others and in dealing with urban pollution problems. Urban and rural activists alike conceded that the left was much more conciliatory and concerned, in or out of power, than the LDP (Liberal Democratic Party). If we look at the effect of political attitudes on partisanship (see Table 4), we note the highly significant finding that the attitudes of switchers were almost identical to those of reformist standpatters. It would appear that these switchers experienced profound disappointment and shock when they realized that some of those whom they had always supported with trust and

---

[17]These measures represent evaluations based on environmental problems and thus acquired through the activist experience. For specific questions and methods of index construction, see Appendix B.

TABLE 3

HOSTILITY TOWARD POLITICAL OBJECTS AMONG RURAL AND
URBAN ANTIPOLLUTION ACTIVISTS

Scales	Rural ($N=24$)	Urban ($N=40$)
A. Attitude toward Right	-1.92	-1.95
B. Attitude toward Left	+1.25	+ .05
C. Net Preference for Left	+1.59	+1.00
D. Hostility toward Politics	- .34	- .95
E. Attitude toward Local Mayor	-1.26	+ .47
F. Attitude toward Prefectural Governor	-1.40	+2.03

NOTE: For Tables 3-5, each scale (A, B, C, D, E, F) runs from -3 (an extremely negative attitude) through 0 (a neutral attitude) to +3 (an extremely enthusiastic attitude). Entries signify mean scale scores. For items included in the scales, see Appendix B.

A. *Attitude toward Right: toward all conservative and obviously right-wing political referents.*

B. *Attitude toward Left: toward all reformist and obviously left-wing political referents.*

C. *Net preference for Left: derived from subtracting Scale A from Scale B, or (B-A)/2, with a negative score indicating a net preference for the right and a positive score indicating a net preference for the left.*

D. *Hostility toward Politics: toward all political referents of right and left, derived from adding Scales A and B, or (A+B)/2, with a negative score indicating a dislike for politics and a positive score indicating a positive feeling toward politics.*

confidence were unscrupulous. Much to their surprise and chagrin, it was the left--the JSP, the JCP, and certain regional labor union federations--that provided aid and comfort. It is extremely significant that switchers arrived at these political attitudes

TABLE 4

HOSTILITY ACCORDING TO CHANGES IN PARTISANSHIP
AMONG ANTIPOLLUTION ACTIVISTS

Scales*	Conservative Standpatters	Switchers	Reformist Standpatters
A. Attitude toward Right	- .29	-2.38	-2.41
B. Attitude toward Left	- .57	+ .69	+ .84
C. Net Preference for Left	- .14	+1.54	+1.62
D. Hostility toward Politics	- .43	- .85	- .79

For description of scales, see note accompanying Table 3, above.

on the basis of real experience, in spite of their predispositions and not because of them. The reformist standpatters' attitudes (intense hostility toward the right and a relatively greater preference for the left) seem to have matched their experience in citizens' movements, but the conservative standpatters seem to have protected their partisan identification by insulating themselves with rather neutral attitudes toward politics.

The attitudes of conservative standpatters become clearer when we note in Table 5 the differential effects of participation in rural and urban movements on political attitudes and on partisan switching. Even conservative standpatters in rural areas became favorable toward the left due to their experience, and in spite of the inertia in their partisan identification (remaining conservative), they shared a preference with the reformists for the left over the right. Conservative standpatters in urban areas, on the other hand, seem to have held on to their identities as conservatives because of an unabated hatred of the left (they could also refer more easily to the inadequacies of local leftist administrations)--but not out of any great love for the political right.

In sum, a very important result of participation in antipollution movements is that activists do conceive that there is a link between their concern with the pollution issue and their partisanship. Although we frequently hear that the reformist parties attract support on the basis of issues from the urban public, it is clear that the parochial and rural activists are capable of being disillusioned and of switching party support on the basis of issue orientation.

TABLE 5

POLITICAL HOSTILITY ACCORDING TO RESIDENCE AND
CHANGES IN PARTISANSHIP

Scales*	Conservative Standpatters		Disillusioned Switchers		Reformist Standpatters	
	Rural (*N*=4)	Urban (*N*=10)	Rural (*N*=7)	Urban (*N*=6)	Rural (*N*=13)	Urban (*N*=24)
A. Attitude toward Right	- .50	- .20	-2.29	-2.50	-2.15	-2.54
B. Attitude toward Left	+1.25	-1.30	+1.14	+ .17	+1.31	+ .58
C. Net Preference for Left	+ .88	- .55	+1.72	+1.34	+1.73	+1.56
D. Hostility toward Politics	+ .38	- .75	- .58	-1.17	- .42	- .98

For description of scales, see note accompanying Table 3, above.

THE PARTICIPANT CITIZEN

If we move from a consideration of political attitudes and partisanship to the question of abstract political beliefs and information levels, we find that urban activists are considerably more democratically inclined than rural activists. This concurs with results from other studies of urban-rural differences (see Richardson, 1974) with the important qualification that environmental activism functions as a catalyst for accelerating belief change among the rural activists. Rural activists were somewhat less interested than urbanites in democratic principles. Presumably this was due to their greater attachment to tradition in general, to their greater initial political

conservatism, to their lack of exposure to abstract political
concepts and to nontraditional political ideals, and to their
lower education levels (for more detailed discussion of this
point, see McKean 1974: Chapter 4). Similarly, rural activists
were much more likely to place value on group efforts rather than
individual action to achieve their goals (see Table 6). Rural
Japanese are still more thoroughly socialized than urbanites
into the traditional emphasis on the power of the group, and
they are also more likely to have doubts about their ability to
navigate in a complex modern society. (As has almost always been
true in both developing and industrial societies, rural residents
in Japan feel a combined sense of inferiority, admiration, envy,
awe, and distaste for urban life, and big cities are popularly
regarded as the center of what is sophisticated, complex, con-
fusing, and mystifying to country people.)

    The gap between rural and urban activists in terms of poli-
tical beliefs paralleled the gap in general information levels.
Urban activists were the more highly informed and aware of their
general surroundings, and were equipped with veritable arsenals
of scientific data and research materials about pollution problems
(see Table 7). It is commonplace to point out that these kinds of
rural-urban differences with respect to political beliefs and
information levels result at least in part from differential
rates of modernization and change. But the picture is not so
simple. The rural activists had a very personal, specialized interest in their own case of pollution and were usually well informed about that particular variety of pollution. They were
also very interested and quite well informed about local elections
and candidates, the political aspects of their own specific problems, and local affairs, precisely because of their involvement
in citizens' movements (see McKean 1974: Chapter 10). Furthermore, rural activists consistently reported having learned a
great deal from the experience of participation. Thus, membership in antipollution movements can have the effect of telescoping
what would usually be a protracted process of attitude change,
from "parochial" to "participant" citizenship, into a period of
a few weeks or months for rural activists. It would appear that
participation in antipollution movements functioned to close the
urban-rural gap in beliefs and information by giving rural activists both the incentive and the occasion to learn about politics
and particular issues, and by serving as a concrete experience in
which democratic values were actually useful.

TABLE 6

POLITICAL BELIEFS AMONG RURAL AND
URBAN ANTIPOLLUTION ACTIVISTS

Item	Rural %	Urban %
WHAT IS THE IDEAL RELATIONSHIP BETWEEN GOVERNMENT AND PEOPLE?		
government on the basis of popular initiative	52	71
government and people in equal positions	44	26
people rely on government guidance	4	3
Total	100%	100%

$(N = 64)$
$Tau\ b = .190*$
$p = .025$

Item	Rural %	Urban %
CAN PEOPLE ACT INDIVIDUALLY ABOUT POLLUTION PROBLEMS OR MUST THEY WAIT FOR GOVERNMENT AND INDUSTRY TO TAKE ACTION FIRST? (open-ended response)		
individual action futile (gave 2 reasons)	4	0
individual action futile (gave 1 reason)	33	10
individual action futile (gave no details)	17	8
individual action worthwhile (mentioned 1 way)	25	28
individual action worthwhile (mentioned 2 ways)	4	23
individual action worthwhile (mentioned 3 ways)	17	23
individual action worthwhile (4 or more ways)	0	10
Total	100%	102%

$(N = 64)$
$Tau\ b = .333$
$p = .001$

*See note, Table 1.

TABLE 7

INFORMATION AND POLITICAL AWARENESS AMONG RURAL AND
URBAN ANTIPOLLUTION ACTIVISTS

Item	Rural %	Urban %	
POLLUTION ISSUE INFORMATION INDEX*			
low	4	0	
medium low	17	0	
medium	38	43	
medium high	29	48	
high	13	10	
Total	101%	101%	$(N = 64)$
			$Tau\ b = .183**$
			$p = .025$
OF THE FOLLOWING, WHICH ARE YOU MOST CONCERNED ABOUT?			
local politics	45	36	
prefectural politics	10	21	
national politics	45	42	
Total	100%	99%	$(N=53)$
AFTER JOINING THIS GROUP, HAVE YOUR POLITICAL OPINIONS, OR IDEAS ABOUT POLITICAL ACTIVITY, OR YOUR GENERAL OPINIONS ABOUT SOCIAL ACTIVITY CHANGED? (Respondents who mentioned learning about law and politics)			
no mention	42	65	
mentioned learning once	25	18	
mentioned learning twice	13	13	
mentioned learning three times	21	5	
Total	101%	101%	$(N = 64)$
			$Tau\ b = -.234$
			$p = .002$

*See Appendix B for descriptions of items.
**See note, Table 1.

CONCLUSIONS

We have demonstrated that there is much variety among citizens' movements, particularly between urban and rural movements, and that citizens' movements are not a single uniform phenomenon. The cultural concomitants of urbanization have shaped protest in middle class residential areas of the big cities, but elsewhere--in more rural areas and in lower class areas of downtown Tōkyō (and presumably of the older cities in general)--organized protest has evolved out of narrower, more parochial concerns, strongly influenced by the traditional attitudes of the surrounding community and the hostile reactions of conservative local governments.

This observation leads us to two further points. First of all, perhaps the traditional-modern dichotomy, or the "rural-urban gap," just is not as significant any more in Japan as it's cracked up to be. To be sure, the gap itself is real: rural areas in Japan *are* repositories of relatively more traditional values, and urbanization *does* introduce different kinds of values which displace some of the old ones. But this fact does not rule out certain fundamental continuities of function and behavior. Citizens' movements can emerge from "traditional" or parochial settings in both rural and urban areas and can acquire characteristics which we often label "modern." Both urban and rural (or, to slice it in a slightly different direction, both sophisticated and parochial, or both modern and traditional) Japanese are capable of defending their own interests and protecting what is precious to them. We should not allow our terms to deceive us. Although these pairs of terms are convenient, they are mutually exclusive opposites only as ideal types, and not in reality where they can quite often exist together.

This leads us to the second point, that participation in citizens' movements produces what we have called a pattern of convergence in the political attitudes and beliefs of rural and urban activists, even though their original circumstances and day-to-day experiences differ a great deal. Because rural movements (often the most traditional in orientation and style at the outset) usually operate in unfriendly surroundings, they frequently undertake an exhaustive search for new methods of articulating their grievances and of influencing policy. The necessity to experiment with new tactics on a trial-and-error basis serves as a practical education in the resources available to citizens in a democracy. Thus environmental problems function as the original stimulus and citizens' movements as the catalyst for greater acceptance of democratic precepts and understanding of the tools of citizenship.

It remains to place these developments in proper perspective. Citizens' movements are not about to coalesce into a uni-
fied national opposition interested in challenging the conservative party's dominance of over 20 years at the national level.
Not only are they limited by the concerns of their members to
having direct influence only at the local level of government,
but activists of all varieties believe that politics at the national level is too remote and, moreover, too impervious to
change in any way to be a worthwhile focus of attention for
citizens' movements. Activists are not revealing any lack of
stamina or sense of purpose here but are probably being hard-
headed realists about what little they might accomplish if they
turned their efforts toward the central government. Not only
are they more successful if they confine themselves to the local
arena, but in the long run the efforts of citizens' movements to
democratize the character of local politics may be a far more
significant contribution to substantive political change in Japan
than a switch in party control at the national level.

APPENDIX A

THE SIZE AND SCOPE OF CITIZENS' MOVEMENTS IN JAPAN

On May 21, 1973, *Asahi Shimbun* reported that citizens' movements already numbered at least 3,000. According to conservative estimates made in an article drawing on this *Asahi* data (see "Citizens' Movements" in Appendix B), the average group has about 20 to 30 core members and perhaps 300 to 500 rank and file members. This would permit us to conclude that at any particular moment there are from 60,000 to 90,000 active adults and from 900,000 to 1,500,000 rank and file participants in citizens' movements. An earlier but equally detailed survey of movements conducted in November 1970 (reported in "Zenkoku no Shimin Undō" [Citizens' Movements Across the Nation], *Shimin*, 1[March, 1971], supplement pp. 1-82) indicated that the average group, *excluding* coalitions, contained 45 core members and 2,000 rank and file participants. These figures would lead us to the even more generous conclusion that about 135,000 adults had already been very active in citizens' movements by 1973, along with 6 million more peripheral participants. Whatever the actual numbers may be, there is no doubt that hundreds of thousands of Japanese have been intimately involved in these movements and that millions more have observed their rapid rise and local successes at close quarters. According to a Tōkyō survey reported in *Asahi Shimbun* (June 15, 1973), 23% said that there had been a movement active in their area during the previous year, and 44% of these respondents had participated in their local movement, indicating that in just one short year as many as 10% of *all* Tōkyōites had been activists in citizens' movements. Furthermore, citizens' movements have definitely established themselves as a respectable form of political activity even among non-participants. The same survey revealed that 68% of the Tōkyōites who had *not* had a local movement to join would nonetheless be inclined to participate if a citizens' movement did take form in their area.

APPENDIX B

INDEX CONSTRUCTION

I. The Sophistication Index (Table 1)

The Sophistication Index was composed of the following variables:

A. *level of education (high education given a positive score)*

B. *protest experience (prior experience given a positive score)*

Based on responses to an open-ended question, "Other than this group, have you ever participated in any group in this neighborhood or district--political, social, or otherwise?" and to follow-up questions on reasons for membership, duration of membership, and level of involvement for each of the groups mentioned. Only protest groups were counted toward a score for this variable.

C. *direct experience with pollution (high score given to respondents interested purely in prevention, who lacked direct contact with pollution)*

Based on responses to two open-ended questions, "Why did you develop interest in the problem that this group is most concerned about?" and "Did anyone you know experience damage directly?"

D. *anticipated gains from antipollution activity (high score given to respondents with altruistic, as opposed to self-interested, involvement)*

Based on an interviewer assessment of the total interview, but usually on responses to the open-ended question, "Why did you develop interest in the problem that this group is most concerned about?"

E. *group concerns (high score given to all respondents in groups with general, as opposed to narrow, objectives and interests)*

Based on an interviewer assessment of all interviews from each particular group.

F. *group involvement in litigation (high score given to respondents from groups not involved in pollution litigation)*

This anomalous scoring is a result of the fact that involvement in antipollution litigation is negatively related to all of the above measures, because it signifies that a group has had little success with other techniques, and in fact has been driven to the courts as a last resort, whereas other groups succeeded with lesser methods, often because of the higher level of political skills they already had. This variable should not be interpreted to represent knowledge of the legal system which an activist brings to his group, although activists who eventually become involved in pollution lawsuits do acquire great familiarity with the legal system as a result of activism, in spite of their other characteristics labelled here as "unsophisticated."

II. Indices Measuring Attitudes toward Political Objects of the Left and Right (Tables 3-5)

Three questions asking respondents to evaluate an assortment of political objects (see below), providing a total of forty different replies per respondent, provided the basis for creating several indices of political attitudes.

Evaluations of the LDP, Prime Minister Tanaka, Prime Minister Satō, and prefectural governors and local mayors who respondents identified as conservative were used to create the index measuring Attitudes toward the Right. Evaluations of the JSP, the JCP, labor unions, and prefectural governors and local mayors whom respondents identified as reformists were used to create the index called Attitudes toward the Left. These two indices were then used to create the indices measuring Net Preference for the Left and Hostility toward Politics (*i.e.,* toward both left and right), as explained in Table 3 in the text.

First, all scales were coded in the same direction from negative attitudes to positive attitudes, and the scores were then summed with an adjustment to allow for the inclusion of extra comments and evaluations mentioned elsewhere in the interview, particularly in reply to open-ended questions about elections, coded on the same four-point rating scale described below. These summed 100-point scales were then collapsed into seven categories, preserving midpoints to represent neutral evaluations. For purposes of presentation here, the seven-point scores were converted into scales running from -3 through 0 (neutrality) to +3, and mean

scores were calculated. Although these manipulations theoreti-
cally require the use of interval level data, it is hoped that
collapsing the final scale into seven broad categories, each
represented by simple integers, does not distort the ordinal
rankings of respondents on these attitudinal dimensions.

A. *Pollution Rating Scale*
    What do you think the attitudes of the [list of 13
    groups] is toward pollution, especially toward the
    problem your group is concerned with? (single
    closed response)
    (1) avoiding the problem is to their advantage
    *   (they think only of their own wealth and power)*
    (2) they often are simply talking about the problem,
    *   but they're disinclined to act, and they're often*
    *   dependent on people who do not want to face the*
    *   problem of pollution, so they avoid concrete acti-*
    *   vities*
    (3) sincere, but various obstacles interfere with
    *   their activity (such as the lack of technical*
    *   understanding, or the fact that others won't co-*
    *   operate with them, or the lack of funds, or the*
    *   fact that the problem is very complex and serious)*
    (4) earnest about solving the problem, active, and
    *   trying as much as possible to discover concrete*
    *   techniques*

B. *Obstacles to Solutions*
    What kind of obstacles make antipollution activity dif-
    ficult for the [same list of 13 groups]? (open-ended
    question, later coded into categories devised as fol-
    lows to provide for the range in replies that respon-
    dents themselves created; phrases and wording are
    the respondents' own) [Note: All respondents who sup-
    plied a "4" answer on the Rating Scale above and said
    nothing unfavorable received the most positive score
    ("7") here as well. All those who gave a rating above of
    1, 2, or 3, and all those who gave a rating of "4" but
    supplemented it with a critical comment were coded here
    according to the obstacles and criticisms mentioned.]
    (1) in a tone of anger or disgust: they find it not
    *   profitable, even destructive to their power or*
    *   profit to pay attention to pollution; they are un-*
    *   scrupulous and tyrannical.*
    (2) in a tone of anger or disgust: they take bribes
    *   from pro-pollution forces; they are tied to industry;*
    *   they get their money from people who don't care.*

(3) *in a tone of anger or disgust: they aren't inter-*
ested; they lack sincerity; they're irresponsible;
they lack principles; they worry only about them-
selves; they are easily pressured into doing others'
bidding; they avoid the issue; they blindly obey
their superiors; they only pretend to help us but
abuse the movement for their own power.

(4) *in a tone of sympathy: they are powerless to act*
and are dependent on others, and being powerless
isn't their fault so much as it is the fault of the
situation itself; they are part of the capitalist
system and can't help it; they are afraid of losing
their jobs or functions.

(5) *in a tone of sympathy: they don't think very hard;*
they can't or don't understand the problem; they
don't see the problem themselves yet; they are un-
realistic; they see development and industry as
desirable goals.

(6) *in a tone of sympathy: they are weak, disunited,*
lack money, have no practice at this, are only the
opposition and can't do much.

(7) *there are no obstacles; they help us and work hard*
for us.

C. *Rating of Actual Experience*
Are you ever worried about any of the following groups
[a different list of 14 groups] trying to damage your
group or use your group for their own purposes? (open-
ended question with coding devised later to reflect the
descriptions which respondents volunteered)
(1) *they hurt us*
(2) *most of them hurt us*
(3) *half and half*
(4) *most of them helped us*
(5) *they helped us*

III. *Pollution Issue Information Index (Table 7, first part)*

The questionnaire contained a battery of 26 questions con-
cerning nine specific environmental problems--garbage, sun-
shine rights, urban density, air pollution, rural develop-
ment, industrial pollution, economic growth, the destruction
of nature, and population. Responses in each of these nine
subject areas were coded according to the level of informa-
tion they revealed--with a "1" signifying that the respon-
dent had demonstrated ignorance of terms or erroneous
information, "3" indicating that the respondent was well

equipped with detailed knowledge, and "2" for all responses
(other than actual missing data) which could not definitely
be labelled either ignorant or informed.

In addition to these nine scores, each respondent was also
assigned a score to reflect general information levels
about pollution, in order to allow for those who had demonstrated in the course of the interview particular ignorance
or knowledge about an environmental issue not included in
the questionnaire battery. These 10 scores were then
summed, and the resulting scale was collapsed into five
categories with an attempt to preserve the "purity" of the
lowest and highest scores, rather than to distribute the
cases evenly across the five collapsed categories. Because
this sample did possess considerable detailed information
about environmental problems, obviously the mean score
earned by the sample as a whole on the index is considerably
higher than the arithmetic midpoint of the index.

REFERENCES

Ackoff, Russell L. *The Design of Social Research.* Chicago: University of Chicago Press, 1953.

Asahi Shinbun (Tōkyō), May 21, 1973; June 15, 1973.

Fukutake, Tadashi. *Japanese Rural Society.* Ithaca, N.Y.: Cornell University Press, 1967.

Gotō Kōten. *Ichikabu Undō no Susume* (Encouragement of the Single-Share Movement). Tōkyō: Perikansha, 1971.

Japan Times (Tōkyō), Dec. 14, 1970; Jan. 10, 1973; May 15, 1973; June 5, 1973; March 29, 1974; Dec. 14, 1974; June 11, 1975; Aug. 21, 1975; Aug. 27, 1975; and Sept. 3, 1975.

Jūmin ni yori Keiji Baipasu Kōgai Kenkyū gurūpu (Residents' Pollution Research Group on the Kyōto-Shiga Bypass). *Kōgai Yosoku to Taisaku* (Pollution: Forecasts and Countermeasures). Tōkyō: Asahi Shimbunsha, 1971.

Kankyōchō. *Kankyō Hakusho* (White Paper on The Environment). Tōkyō: Ōkurashō, 1972.

Matsubara Haruo. *Kōgai to Chiiki Shakai: Seikatsu to Jūmin Undō no Shakaigaku* (Pollution and Regional Society: The Sociology of Livelihood and Residents' Movements). Tōkyō: Nihon Keizai Shimbunsha, 1971.

Matsushita Ryūichi. *Kazanashi no Onnatachi: Aru Gyoson no Tatakai* (The Women of Kazanashi: The Struggle of a Fishing Village). Tōkyō: Asahi Shimbunsha, 1972.

McKean, Margaret A. "The Potential for Grass-Roots Democracy in Postwar Japan: The Anti-Pollution Movement as a Case Study in Political Activism." Unpublished Ph.D. Dissertation, University of California, Berkeley, 1974.

Miyamoto Ken'ichi. "Jūmin Undō no Riron to Rekishi" (The Theory and History of Residents' Movements). In Miyamoto Ken'ichi and Endō Akira, editors. *Toshi Mondai to Jūmin Undō* (Urban Problems and Residents' Movements), Volume 8: *Gendai Nihon no Toshi Mondai* (Urban Problems in Modern Japan. Kyōto: Sekibunsha, 1971.

Nie, Norman H., et al. *Statistical Package for the Social Sciences.* Second Edition. New York: McGraw-Hill, 1975.

"Peasant Uprisings and Citizens' Revolts." *Japan Interpreter*,
8:3 (Autumn, 1973), 279-83.

Richardson, Bradley. *The Political Culture of Japan*. Berkeley:
University of California Press, 1974.

Siegel, Sidney. *Nonparametric Statistics for the Behavioral
Sciences*. New York: McGraw-Hill, 1956.

Shimin (Tokyo), March, 1971, No. 1.

Shoji Hikaru, and Miyamoto Ken'ichi. *Osorubeki Kōgai* (Fearful
Pollution). Tokyo: Iwanami shoten, 1964.

Smith, Constance, and Anne Freedman. *Voluntary Associations:
Perspectives on the Literature*. Cambridge: Harvard University Press, 1972.

Sōrifu (The Prime Minister's Office). "Kōgai Mondai" (Pollution
Problems). (Gekkan) *Yoron Chōsa*, 4:6 (June, 1972), 2-28.

Tsuru Shigeto. *Gendai Shihon Shugi to Kōgai* (Modern Capitalism
and Pollution). Tokyo: Iwanami shoten, 1968.

Ui Jun. *Kōgai no Seijigaku: Minamata Byō wo Megutte* (The Politics of Pollution: On Minamata Disease). Tokyo: Sanseidō, 1968.

_____. *Kōgai Genron* (A Discussion on Pollution), Vols. I,II,
III. Tokyo: Aki shobo, 1971a, 1971b, and 1971b.

FURTHER READINGS IN ENGLISH

"Citizens' Movements." *Japan Quarterly*, 20:4 (October-December,
1973), 368-73.

Glickman, Norman J. "Conflict over Public Facility Location in
Japan." *Area Development in Japan*, 6(1972), 20-43.

Huddle, Norie, Michael Reich, and Nahum Stiskin. *Island of
Dreams: Environmental Crisis in Japan*. Tokyo: Autumn
Press, 1975.

Kuroda Yasumasa. "Protest Movements in Japan: A New Politics."
Asian Survey, 12:11 (November, 1972), 947-52.

Matsushita, Keiichi. "Politics of Citizen Participation." *Japan Interpreter,* 9:4 (Spring, 1975), 451-64.

"Pollution Case Law." *Japan Quarterly,* 20:3 (July-September, 1973), 251-55.

Reich, Michael, and Norie Huddle. "Pollution and Social Response." *Area Development in Japan,* 7 (1973), 34-47.

Simcock, Bradford L. "Environmental Pollution and Citizens' Movements: The Social Sources and Significance of Anti-Pollution Protest in Japan." *Area Development in Japan,* 5 (1972), 13-22.

Steiner, Kurt, Ellis Krauss, and Scott Flanagan, editors. *Local Opposition in Japan: Progressive Local Governments, Citizens' Movements, and National Politics (forthcoming),* particularly articles by Lewis, McKean, and Simcock on citizens' movements.

Thurston, Donald R. "Aftermath in Minamata." *Japan Interpreter* 9:1 (Spring, 1974), 25-42.

"Tokyo's Garbage War." *Japan Quarterly,* 19:2 (April-June, 1972), 125-29.

Tsurutani, Taketsugu. "A New Era of Japanese Politics: Tokyo's Gubernatorial Election." *Asian Survey,* 12:5 (May, 1972), 429-43.

Ui Jun, "The Singularities of Japanese Pollution." *Japan Quarterly,* 19:3 (July-September, 1972), 281-91.

Above, view of plaza in front of Okayama Station, 1953. Below, same view in 1970.
Photos courtesy of Professor David H. Kornhauser, Department of Geography, University of
Hawaii at Manoa.

V

SOCIAL CHANGE AND COMMUNITY INVOLVEMENT IN METROPOLITAN JAPAN

*James W. White**

INTRODUCTION

The foregoing papers have offered a series of microcosmic views of particular instances of the workings of the forces of social and economic change in urban Japan, and of the implications of these changes for the political attitudes and behavior of urban Japanese. These cases are not unique; they are simply examples of the following macrophenomena which, although in many of their aspects are not new to Japan, have comprised during the postwar generation an unprecedented syndrome of change:

Demographic change: migration rates of over 8% of the nation's population each year (Kuroda, 1973), and especially heavy flows of population between cities, from the cities to the suburbs, and into the *danchi*.

Changes in social relationships resulting from such demographic change: transience, flux, and increasing opportunities and freedom which can be seen either as liberating or deracinating by those involved.

New social cleavages: as newcomers move into older communities and as youngsters grow up with values foreign to their elders.

Industrialization and its attendant pollution: all Japanese cities are affected to some extent. Even where pollution is not

---
*The author gratefully acknowledges the donors of the financial support which made this study possible: the Ford Foundation, the Social Science Research Council, the Carolina Population Center, the University of North Carolina Research Council, the University of North Carolina Comparative Urban Studies Program, and the Japan Foundation. Once the data were gathered, Ms. Bing Lau's coding and Morse Kalt's programming and data preparation were equally important, and equally appreciated.

a major problem, the "modernization" of which industrialization
is a part has also brought urban infrastructural developments--
highways, rail lines, airports, subways, and so forth--which can
have similarly disruptive or debilitating effects.

*Increasing permeability of the boundaries of the intra-
urban community:* the distance between the locus of neighborhood
problems and the arena where they can be solved increases continually.

These papers have also sketched out many of the features
of another, more general phenomenon that has been recognized in
urban studies literature the world over, that is, the general decline of the urban community. Some of its features are as follows:

Attitudinal change: urbanites seem increasingly apathetic
and cynical about their neighborhoods; interest in, commitment
to, and identification with the neighborhood is on the wane; and
there is a new emphasis on individual rights, the quality of personal life, and the nuclear family at the expense of any larger
collectivity.

Social changes bringing new issues and needs: new political cleavages have emerged which established communities and community leaders are unable to handle.

New social and political conditions: residential atomization and governmental centralization, both inimical to the assump-
tions of participant democracy, have spread.

Participation in community life: many aspects of community
life, including long-established community organizations such as
the *chōkai* or *chōnaikai*, are losing their appeal to residents.

Decreased political relevance: the overall political relevance of the intracity political community has decreased as its
boundaries become more permeable and its problems are no longer
susceptible of solution within its borders or through its own
resources.

New forms of political organization and participation: new
forms of political organization and participation in the cities--
electoral and nonelectoral, violent and nonviolent--have emerged.

The analysis below will explicitly exclude several matters
otherwise deserving of treatment. First, *the efforts of this paper*

will be restricted to the neighborhood level and will largely ignore the higher levels of metropolitan government. Second, since Frank Munger's introduction focuses specifically upon them, cross-national comparisons will be avoided for the most part. Most egregiously, intraurban comparisons will be excluded. To generalize about "the city" or "city life" or even such areas as "the suburbs" in any country is risky, and Tōkyō itself merits division into a number of analytically separable regions. However, as this monograph is concerned with the neighborhood level, we have proceeded to consider the urban neighborhood in Tōkyō as a whole.

NEIGHBORHOOD CONCERN AND PARTICIPATION

Given the "decline of community" witnessed in many of the great cities of the world and suggested in these papers, it seems possible that the urban neighborhood in Japan may disintegrate as a meaningful political entity; however, the foregoing papers indicate changes in direction rather than disintegration.[1] Nevertheless, despite visible developments in some Japanese cities-- citizens' and consumers' movements, product "user unions," the adoption of "citizen participation" as a goal of the present Tōkyō metropolitan administration, and the recall movements threatened or executed in consequence of local crises--*the future of the urban community seems, at best, mixed from the point of view of popular democratic theory.*

Given this perspective, we have analyzed a body of survey data obtained in three neighborhoods (*chō* or *machi*) in Tōkyō in 1972.[2] The areas sampled--one central city (*shitamachi*), one urban residential (*yamanote*), and one suburban--are broadly representative of the major regions of the metropolis.[3] The sample, 839 persons aged 15-60, resembles the population of Tōkyō as a

---

[1]This "decline" was hypothesized in greatest detail perhaps by the "Chicago School" of sociologists (see James White, "Political Aspects of Internal Migration" in Internal Migration in Industrial Societies, ed. by George Myers /Durham: Duke University Press, forthcoming7). For recent examinations of the American case, see Roland Warren, The Community in America (Chicago: Rand McNally, 1972); and Sidney Verba and Norman Nie, Participation in America (New York: Harper and Row, 1972), ch. 13.

[2]See Appendix A for a description of the study.

[3]For some justifications of and precedents for the selection, see Tōkyō-to, Sōmu-kyoku, Tōkei-bu, Jinkō no Ugoki (Population Movement) Tōkyo (annual); Kurasawa Susumu, Nihon no Toshi Shakai (Japanese Urban Society) (Tōkyō: Fukumura, 1968); Isomura Eiichi et al., Toshi Keisei no Ronri to Jūmin (Urban Residents and the Logic of City Formation) (Tōkyō: Tōkyō University Press, 1971); Kokumin Seikatsu Shingikai, ed., Komyunitei (Community) (Tōkyō: Ōkura-sho, 1970); Tōkyō Shisei Chōsa Kai, Tōkyō ni okeru Chiiki Shakai Sochiki (Local Social Organizations in Tōkyō) (Tōkyō: Tōkyō Shisei Chōsa Kai, 1971); and R.P. Dore, City Life in Japan (Berkeley: University of California Press, 1967).

New residential housing in suburban Tōkyō with cabbage patch in foreground. Photo by James W. White.

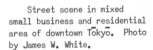

Street scene in mixed small business and residential area of downtown Tōkyō. Photo by James W. White.

whole almost exactly in age and sex structure. Given the age limits of the sample, the approximation to the Tokyo populace in educational attainment is fairly close, although there is some overrepresentation of white-collar and higher-income groups.

These data will be used to test three hypotheses dealing with attitudinal and behavioral neighborhood involvement. A profile of the neighborhood participant will then be presented, and finally, on a collective level, suggestions of some of the functions--political, administrative, and social--being served by the local community in urban Japan.

PARTICIPATION IN THE *DANCHI*

A wide variety of judgments, both empirical and impressionistic, have fostered the image of the *danchi* resident as an anonymous individual, known only to his company and family, who knows little and cares less about the neighborhood in which he lives. Christie Kiefer's paper aptly describes the complexity of the *danchi* and its lifestyles and goes beyond such simplism. In contrast to Kiefer's findings, other researchers have noted the paradoxically high frequency of voluntary socializing, satisfaction with neighborhood as a place to live, citizen concerns, and proclivity to act out political dissatisfaction found in some *danchi*.[4] Nevertheless, one still comes away with the impression that the *danchi* people are a pretty weak reed, from the perspective of those who would build viable political communities within the city. The data presented here confirm this impression (see Table 1).

To test the first hypothesis, that *danchi residence affects neighborhood involvement,* the sample was divided into groups of home owners, apartment dwellers, and residents of two *shataku* (company-owned *danchi*). Eleven measures were created to test residents' concern for, commitment to, interest and participation in, and satisfaction and interaction with their neighborhoods. On 7 of the 11 measures the *shataku* residents scored "worse" than other apartment dwellers, who in turn scored "worse" than home owners. On two of the measures (Nos. 10 and 11), home owners scored "better" than renters of both kinds, and on the two remaining measures (Nos. 3 and 5) no statistically significant relationship is apparent. In many cases no group appears impressively participant or concerned, but the overall picture is clear: Neighborhoods characterized by large influxes of *danchi* residents (unless the influx is so large that the *danchi* itself becomes a new neighborhood, as in Kiefer's case) can be expected

---

[4]Kurasawa (1968), pp. 248-55, and "Danchi Jūmin to Jimoto Jūmin" (Danchi Residents and Local Residents), Toshi Mondai, 58:12 (December 1967), p. 55; Isomura et al., p. 238; Chōfu-shi, Sōmu-bu, Kikaku-shitsu, Chōfu Shimin no Ishiki Chōsa Sho (Report on a Survey of Citizens' Attitudes in Chōfu) (Tōkyō: Chōfu-shi, Sōmu-bu, Kikaku-shitsu, 1971), pp. 123ff.

TABLE 1

COMMUNITY INVOLVEMENT OF *DANCHI* DWELLERS, APARTMENT DWELLERS, AND HOMEOWNERS*

Items	Percentage Scoring	*Danchi* Dwellers	Apartment Dwellers	Home Owners	All	*Tau c*	*p* value	*N*
1. Factual knowledge about neighborhood	*LOW* on a 4-point scale	61%	58%	40%	49%	.18	.0000	615
2. Perception of neighborhood cohesion and unity	*NEG.* on 4-point scale	49	34	21	28	.16	.0000	432
3. Satisfaction with neighborhood as a place to live	*HIGH* on 3-point scale	85	47	55	55	-.05	.11 (*n.s.*)	372
4. Desire to move from neighborhood	*YES* on dichotomous scale	59	58	28	42	.31	.0000	574
5. Perceived extent of neighbors' concern with neighborhood problems	*GREAT* on 3-point scale	68	62	66	65	.01	.43 (*n.s.*)	250
6. Proportion of perceived sources of support in time of crisis seen in own neighborhood	*NONE* on 4-point scale	75	67	55	61	.12	.0001	607
7. Does respondent discuss politics with neighbors	*NO* on dichotomous scale	84	75	66	71	.12	.004	430
8. Does respondent get political advice from neighbors	*YES* on dichotomous scale	24	34	41	32	.10	.01	494
9. Extent to which neighbors are friends, and own best friends live in own neighborhood	*HIGH* on 3-point scale	25	31	38	34	.10	.001	614
10. Is respondent a member of a neighborhood association	*YES* on dichotomous scale	28	28	58	41	-.25	.0000	620
11. Has respondent participated in activities of neighborhood problem-solving group	*YES* on dichotomous scale	4	5	13	9	-.08	.0003	620

*The ranking of residential types is assumed to be ordinal here, representing an increasing degree of rootedness in the neighborhood.

to undergo significant changes in their cohesion, social interaction, and potential for political action. Further interviews
of persons in the neighborhood surrounding the *shataku* corrob-
orated this conclusion: The social and political coherence of
the neighborhood had been adversely affected by the emergence of
the two *shataku* and their residents were seen as a pretty useless
crew as far as the neighborhood was concerned.

SOCIAL CLASS AND INVOLVEMENT

Hypothesis 2, which derives from research in many countries
and is echoed in Christie Kiefer's paper, is that *the upper class
constitutes the pillar of democracy, combining a concern for
democratic values with the inclination to participate politically
and the necessary skills (in terms of education, money, sophistication, and leisure time) necessary to participate effectively.*
In the more established, less dynamic areas of Tōkyō--the central
city in general and neighborhoods of shopkeepers and old residences in particular--one might expect this relationship to hold.
However, social class as measured here is of limited help in explaining neighborhood involvement (see Table 2).

To test this hypothesis, I grouped my sample into (a) central city and older commercial and residential areas and (b) suburban sprawl, new residential, and *danchi (shataku)* areas, and
compared them in terms of the influence of social class on 11
measures of neighborhood involvement. The results were these:

1. On one of the measures (perception of cohesion), no
consistent relationship was visible.

2. On six of the eleven (Nos. 2-5, 10, and 11), involvement varied as predicted with social class, but on three (satisfaction and membership and participation in neighborhood organizations) class was about equally influential in both residential
areas, and on three (perceived concern, desire to move, and community knowledge) the effect was greater in the newer, more dynamic areas.

3. On four of the measures (Nos. 6-9), all of which deal
with social interaction, it is the middle groups on the social
scale who appear to be most involved. The pattern is clearer
in the older areas; here, perhaps, the pillar of neighborhood
cohesion is not the upper class but the "old middle class" of
shopkeepers and other small entrepreneurs. In the newer and less
stable neighborhoods, on the other hand, where business connec-
tions and long residence cannot motivate or facilitate participation, it may be that the frequently-assumed participant impulse

TABLE 2

COMMUNITY INVOLVEMENT BY SOCIAL CLASS, IN DIFFERENT TYPES OF NEIGHBORHOODS*

Items	Socioeconomic Status	Newer Neighborhoods and Danchi**				Older Established Neighborhoods[+]			
		Percentage Scoring	Tau c	p value	N	Percentage Scoring	Tau c	p value	N
1. Perception of neighborhood cohesion	1 *LOW* SES	*LOW* (dichot. scale) 80%				*LOW* (dichot. scale) 60%			
	2	75	.09	.10	190	59	-.04	.26	251
	3	78				53			
	4 *HIGH* SES	67				69			
2. Perceived extent of neighbors' concern with neighborhood problems	1 *LOW* SES	*MOST CONCERNED* (3-point scale) 50%				*MOST CONCERNED* (3-point scale) 52%			
	2	80	.11	.04	146	46	.09	.15	109
	3	74				64			
	4 *HIGH* SES	76				60			
3. Desire to move from neighborhood	1 *LOW*	*YES* (dichot. scale) 59%				*YES* (dichot. scale) 45%			
	2	40	.13	.02	275	33	.08	.09	307
	3	49				40			
	4 *HIGH*	38				33			
4. Factual knowledge about neighborhood	1 *LOW*	*LOW* (dichot. scale) 90%				*LOW* (dichot. scale) 94%			
	2	84	.12	.006	295	86	.08	.02	324
	3	84				81			
	4 *HIGH*	72				87			
5. Satisfaction with neighborhood	1 *LOW*	*HIGH* (3-point scale) 57%				*HIGH* (3-point scale) 39%			
	2	56	.12	.02	184	52	.11	.04	191
	3	62				51			
	4 *HIGH*	77				59			
6. Proportion of perceived sources of support in times of crisis in own neighborhood	1 *LOW*	*NONE* (dichot. scale) 93%				*NONE* (dichot. scale) 98%			
	2	94	-.01[††]	.43	294	81	.04[††]	.14	318
	3	92				85			
	4 *HIGH*	95				96			

(cont'd)

Table 2 (cont.)

Items	Socioeconomic Status	Newer Neighborhoods and Danchi				Older Established Neighborhoods			
		Percentage Scoring	Tau c	p value	N	Percentage Scoring	Tau c	p value	N
7. Does respondent discuss politics with neighbors	1 *LOW* SES 2 3 4 *HIGH* SES	*YES* (dichot. scale) 31% 26 28 27	-.03††	.34	218	*YES* (dichot. scale) 19% 46 36 22	.02††	.36	220
8. Does respondent get political advice from neighbors	1 *LOW* SES 2 3 4 *HIGH* SES	*YES* (dichot. scale) 37% 31 29 33	-.03††	.32	239	*YES* (dichot. scale) 35% 52 37 32	-.04††	.30	260
9. Extent to which neighbors are friends and own best friends are in own neighborhood	1 *LOW* 2 3 4 *HIGH*	*LOW* (3-point scale) 43% 38 39 46	.01††	.39	295	*LOW* (3-point scale) 47% 24 33 54	-.04††	.24	324
10. Is respondent a member of a neighborhood association	1 *LOW* 2 3 4 *HIGH*	*YES* (dichot. scale) 34% 46 47 52	-.14	.02	299	*YES* (dichot. scale) 23% 45 49 41	-.18	.001	326
11. Has respondent participated in neighborhood problem-solving organizational activities	1 *LOW* 2 3 4 *HIGH*	*YES* (dichot. scale) 7% 6 9 19	-.09	.01	299	*YES* (dichot. scale) 6% 5 11 16	-.08	.01	326

*Social class, or socioeconomic status (SES) is calculated here by means of a 100-point scale divided into quartiles, incorporating measures of respondent's (a) family income, (b) educational attainment, (c) occupational status, and (d) social status as estimated by interviewer.
**"Newer neighborhoods" includes the entire *machi* in Chofu, and the *danchi* portion in the "uptown," metropolitan residential ward of Shibuya.
†"Older neighborhoods" includes the balance of the *machi* in Shibuya, and the entire *machi* in the central city ward of Sumida.
††The *tau c* should be judged appropriately since there appears to be a lack of monotonicity in the SES scale for this question.

associated with high social status is the only mobilizing factor
at work, thus explaining the greater effect, noted above, of class
in the newer neighborhoods. At any rate, however--and the data
are hardly conclusive--the original hypothesis is not confirmed
in any single instance.

POLITICAL PARTICIPATION AND SEX

A final hypothesis commonly encountered in attempts to explain the political implications of social change in Japan concerns sex roles. Whether by default in the absence of commuter
husbands; by virtue of increasing "my-homeism" coupled with their
heavily family-centered existence; or as a result of labor-saving
appliances, enhanced leisure time, fewer children, and decreasing
social constraints in urban environments, *Japanese women are
generally expanding their political role, especially in the cities
and more particularly in the suburbs and danchi* (Iwai, 1971). The
image is most striking in the suburbs--in many neighborhoods there
simply are no working-age males to be seen during daylight hours
on weekdays. Absentee residents are seldom considered to be
paragons of neighborhood concern, and even if they are concerned,
their absence and frequent fatigue when at home might well lead
to delegation of political chores to housewives.

Some observations, in fact, produce the impression that
the *danchi* and suburbs have become *predominantly* the political
preserve of women; the data presented here do not indicate that
this is so, but do support the above hypothesis and reveal a
striking sexual difference in political participation between
different areas of Tōkyō (see Table 3). Again, dividing the sample into a) central city and older commercial and residential
areas and b) suburban sprawl, new residental, and *danchi (shataku),*
women are compared with men on five measures of political participation, and the hypothesis is supported on four of them.

In "Participation in national elections" and "Number of
forms of political participation done beyond voting" (collabora-
tive work with neighbors on local problems, attendance at political rallies, and campaign participation), the usual Japanese
male-oriented sex bias in participation was significantly smaller
in the suburbs and *danchi*. And in "Participation in local elections" and "Is respondent a member of neighborhood association,"
male dominance in the central city was *reversed* in the suburbs
and *danchi,* with women playing a more active political role.

One must note throughout Table 3 that, although women apparently are more active politically in the suburbs, they do not

TABLE 3

POLITICAL PARTICIPATION BY SEX, IN DIFFERENT TYPES OF NEIGHBORHOODS*

Items	Sex	Newer Neighborhoods and *Danchi* %	N	Older Established Neighborhoods %	N
1. Participation in national elections (% "Always vote")	Male Female	57% 56	297	66% 56	320
2. Participation in local elections (% "Always vote")	Male Female	52 58	289	64 52	320
3. Is respondent a member of neighborhood association (% "Yes")	Male Female	38 49	309	44 32	333
4. Number of forms of political participation beyond voting (% "None")	Male Female	59 64	309	53 73	333

*Categorization of neigbhorhoods same as in Table 2.

appear to dominate any dimension of participation, and are, in
fact, still "inferior" to men on all but two measures (Nos. 2
and 4). Moreover, these data do not permit any strong assertion
regarding the cause of these differences in intracity participation rates. Prior research indicates that freedom--from household drudgery, from ubiquitous and domineering husbands, and
from neighborhood social mores--is the independent variable
which explains female prominence in the suburbs. But whatever
the factors which come between suburbanization and increased participation, it does seem that suburbanization and commutation
are the best things that have happened to the political libera-
tion of Japanese women since the introduction of the vacuum
cleaner.

THE PARTICIPANTS: WHO AND WHY?

The foregoing analysis of neighborhood involvement in the
Japanese city has so far suggested two categories of participants: home owners and housewives. In an effort to present a
fuller picture of the participant profile, eight more characteristics were added to the previous three (sex, social class, and
residence) and the relationship of each to eleven measures of
community involvement grouped under four (intuitive) dimensions
was examined.

Evaluation of the neighborhood as a place to live:

   1) satisfaction with neighborhood;

   2) no desire to move from neighborhood; and

   3) positive perception of neighborhood cohesion.

Social interaction:

   1) many perceived sources of intra-neighborhood support;

   2) discuss politics with neighbors;

   3) solicit political advice from neighbors; and

   4) high in extent to which neighbors are friends and
      vice versa.

Organizational participation:

   1) membership in neighborhood association;

   2) participation in neighborhood problem-solving group
      activities; and

3) contact with public officials concerning neighborhood or group problems.

Factual knowledge of the community:

1) knowledge of neighborhood leaders and problems.

Although the results of this analysis (see Table 4) are
ambiguous, one profile and two sets of explanatory factors
emerge. The clear profile emerges from the Social Interaction dimension and corroborates research done previously (Nakamura, 1967; Kokumin Seikatsu Shingikai, 1970; Tsushima *et al.*,
1960). Those most socially active and integrated tend to be:
women; persons in their 40s and 50s and of middling social class;
merchants, shopkeepers, small entrepreneurs, housewives; people
with relatively little education and with children in elementary
and/or junior high school; home owners who are long-time residents
of the neighborhood; and strong supporters of some political
party.

The two factors that, across several dimensions, appear to
explain active community involvement are a *home owner-parent
grouping* (40-50-year-old home owners with school-age children),
in which long-time residence may also be an element[5]; and *partisanship* (irrespective of which party is supported), in which
strongly partisan individuals registered significant involvement
across all dimensions. To clarify the former factor, a separate
analysis in which 40-50-year-old home-owning parents were compared
as a group with all other respondents showed the group to be
relatively heavily involved on seven of nine measures; as for
the latter, involvement varied with partisanship on nine of ten
measures.[6]

The other dimensions of involvement were ambiguous, creating
suspicion that they do not in fact constitute meaningful dimensions

---

[5]For support of this notion, see Sumida-ku, Kōhō-shitsu, Sumida Kusei Yoron Chōsa (A
Study of Public Opinions Regarding the Sumida Ward Government) (Tōkyō: Sumida Kōhō-shitsu,
1971), pp. 41ff, 57-59, 7-81; Chōfu-shi, p. 127; Yamamoto Noboru, "Shinjū Shimin no Jichi
Ishiki" (Attitudes Regarding Political Autonomy Among New Urbanites), Toshi Mondai 56:5
(May 1965), pp. 19-20. The finding that children increase the cohesive potential of a
neighborhood simply corroborates the Japanese view that "the community whose children play
together stays together (kodomo wa komyunitei no kasugai)." See Kokumin Seikatsu Shingikai,
op. cit.

[6]To a certain extent there is overlap between the homeowner-parents and the strong
partisans (tau b=.16), but this overlap is sufficiently small that any future analysis
would be well advised to treat them separately.

TABLE 4

TYPES OF RESPONDENTS MOST LIKELY TO BE INVOLVED IN COMMUNITY, ON ELEVEN MEASURES OF INVOLVEMENT

DIMENSIONS / Measure of Involvement	Sex	Age	SES*	Occupation**	Education[+]	Children[++]	Home Ownership	Length of Residence[§]	Political Interest[§§]	Traditionalism[△]	Partisanship[△△]
EVALUATION											
1. *High* on satisfaction with neighborhood as a place to live	n.s.[¶]	n.s.	High	White-collar	High	JHS	n.s.	n.s.	--[¶¶]	--	--
2. *No* desire to move from neighborhood	n.s.	50s, teens	High	White-collar, students	Low; High	JHS; elem & JHS	Owners	Long-time residence	n.s.	n.s.	n.s.
3. *Positive* on perception of neighborhood cohesion	Women	50s, teens, & 40s	n.s.	Merchants, managers & wives	Med.	school-age	Owners	Long-time residence	n.s.	n.s.	Strong partisans
KNOWLEDGE											
4. *High* on factual knowledge about neighborhood	n.s.	50s, 40s	High	Managers, White-col., merchants	n.s.	JHS, elem & JHS	Owners	Long-time residence	Strong interest	n.s.	Strong partisans
SOCIAL INTERACTION											
5. *Many* on perceived sources of intra-neighborhood support	Women	50s, 40s	Middle	Merchants, wives	Low	JHS; elem & JHS	Owners	Long-time	n.s.	n.s.	Strong partisan
6. *Yes* on discussion of politics with neighbors	Women	n.s.	Middle	Merchants, wives	Low	JHS; elem & JHS	Owners	Long-time residence	n.s.	Traditionalists	Strong partisans
7. *Yes* on soliciting political advice from neighbors	Women	50s, 40s	n.s.	Merchants, wives	Low	JHS; elem & JHS	Owners	Long-time residence	n.s.	n.s.	Strong partisans
8. *High* in extent to which neighbors are friends, and vice versa	n.s.	50s, 40s	Middle	Merchants, wives, sales	Low	JHS; elem & JHS	Owners	Long-time residence	n.s.	Traditionalists	Strong partisans

(cont'd)

DIMENSIONS Measure of Involvement	Sex	Age	SES*	Occupation**	Education†	Children††	Ownership	Length of Residence§	Political Interest§§	Traditionalism△	Partisanship△△
ORGANIZATIONAL PARTICIPATION											
9. *Yes* on membership in neighborhood association	n.s.	50s, 40s	Mid-dle	Merchants, managers	n.s.	JHS; elem & JHS	Owners	Long-time residence	Strong interest	Traditional-ists	Strong partisans
10. *Yes* on participation in neighborhood problem-solving group activities	n.s.	50s, 40s	High	White-collar	High	JHS; elem & JHS	Owners	Long-time residence	Strong interest	Modernists	Strong partisans
11. *Collective* on whether matter regarding which political official was contacted was personal or neighborhood/group problem¶¶¶	n.s.	20s	High	Workers, (skilled), white-collar	n.s.	Elem.	Owners	5-20 years	n.s.	n.s.	Strong partisans

*A composite index of SES including measures of income, educational attainment, occupational status, and interviewer estimate of respondent's social class.

**Nature of occupation, as opposed to occupational status (manual/nonmanual).

†Included in order to see if education had any independent effect, apart from its inclusion in SES.

††Whether respondent had school-age children (and, if so, what level of school), other children, or no children.

§Length of residence is measured in years. "Longtime residence" means 20 years or more, but less than entire life.

§§A 4-point composite index, including measures of interest in national and metropolitan politics and frequency of political discussions.

△Traditionalism: an additive, 3-point index derived from 2 dichotomous questions dealing with preference for traditional or nontraditional behavior in given situations. (See Hayashi Chikio *et al.* [1970:557,Ques.4.4; 560,Ques.5.6).]

△△A 4-point composite index, including measures of consistency in party support across two elections, strength of support for party, and extent of campaign work for party supported.

¶No significant association at .05.

¶¶No data.

¶¶¶Sample sizes were quite small for this variable (approximately 80-100) and relationships specified are therefore tenuous.

after all, or that the causation of activity in the more complex
or demanding modes of activity is too complex to be elucidated
by an analysis as simple as this. These suspicions are strength-
ened by the inconsistent appearance in some dimensions of other
factors. Social class, for example, does seem related positively
to community knowledge; it relates negatively with social interaction and appears again, as does political interest, as a hypothetically causal factor in the political participation dimension.[7] The resultant suspicion is that social interaction requires less, in terms of initiative, skills, and resources,
than do the other dimensions--perhaps all that is needed is a
desire to fulfill universal human social needs and the opportunities to fulfill them, which physical propinquity permits.
Perhaps, therefore, one might expect that those "handicapped" in
terms of education and income and thus perhaps less cosmopolitan
in their relationships would be more dependent upon their immediate neighborhood than are their social "betters," and would
therefore appear most clearly on a neighboring dimension of social interaction. Similarly, one might expect that many of the
same characteristics which lead to neighboring would be uncon-
nected with the more complex modes of behavior, and that factors
more clearly explanatory of complex behavior would be unrelated
to neighboring.

Overall, few of the relationships uncovered by the analysis
of "participants" were very strong.[8] In other words, although
the causation was sometimes clear, it is equally clear that other factors were also involved. Part of the problem may be individual or local idiosyncrasies, as Margaret McKean suggests:
Movements occur where the pollution occurs, and who participates
may be determined primarily by whose ox is being gored. Method-
ological flaws may mask other relationships: it has been suggested that social class is not as significant a factor in Japan
as in the West or that, if it does operate, it must be measured
in different ways than those used here.[9]

---

[7]One must note, however, the relative weakness of the relationship. See also in this regard Ikeuchi Hajime, ed., <u>Shimin Ishiki no Kenkyū</u> (A Study of Citizen Consciousness)(Tokyo: Tokyo University Press, 1974), pp. 408-12; Sumida-ku, Kōhō-shitsu, pp. 57-59, 74-75.

[8]Among all the linear relationships discovered, only one or two correlated at more than r=.20. Regarding general strength of association between variables, <u>tau b</u>'s were only rarely greater than .20.

[9]The former viewpoint is most strongly presented by Nakane Chie in her <u>Japanese Society</u> (Berkeley: University of California Press, 1970), esp. ch. 3. It is echoed by Watanuki Jōji in "Patterns of Politics in Present-day Japan," in <u>Party Systems and Voter Alignments,</u> ed. by Seymour Lipset and Stein Rokkan (New York: Free Press, 1967), pp. 447-66; although he has since qualified his argument (see "Change and Persistence in Socio-Political Behavior: Japanese Case," unpublished paper, Sophia University, Tōkyō, 1972). The latter viewpoint was elicited from Professor William Cummings of the University of

There remains the difficulty of causal complexity. This
may take the form of psychological complexity--there may be attitudes not included in this analysis which play significant roles
in causing neighborhood involvement. It may take the form of
conditional efficacy of certain factors: the differential effects of sex under residential conditions are one example of
this, as is the paradox of the *danchi* mentioned above.

The paradox of red-hot activism in some *danchi* and complete
apathy in others, atomization in some and gregariousness in others,
has been observed frequently.[10] I would suggest that this con-
tradiction is the result of the interaction of residence and social class, especially as social class reflects mobility expectations. There are two broad types of *danchi* inhabitants: those
for whom the apartment is a way station on the road to a home
of their own (the people of whom Christie Kiefer writes), and
those (generally blue-collar) for whom the *danchi* constitutes an
objective--the top rung of their personal mobility ladder. The
first type of person tends to tolerate the *danchi*--barely--with
the knowledge that it is a temporary residence; he concentrates
on getting by and getting out. The second type of person concentrates on making the *danchi* a place that fits his or her residential ideal: a place in which social needs are met, human
gratification obtained, and the environment cared for and enhanced. In short, such people tend to try to make the *danchi* a
community.

Data from a study of the Tama New Town on the outskirts of
Tōkyō support this hypothesis.[11] Tama includes both blue- and
white-collar *danchi* and, relative to the white-collar group, the
lower-income, lower-class *danchi* people:

1) improved their residential conditions most by moving
   to Tama;

2) felt the most improvement and were most satisfied with
   having made the move;

3) had stronger feelings of entering a new community, not
   "just another *danchi*";

[9](cont.) Chicago in several communications in early 1975. An analysis of both positions appears in James White, "Social Status and Political Participation in Tokyo," unpublished paper, University of North Carolina, Chapel Hill, 1975.

[10] For a summary of the discussion, see Kurasawa, pp. 55ff.

[11] Tōkyō-to Minami-tama Shintoshi Kaihatsu Hombu, Tama Nyū Taun Kyojūsha no Jū-seikatsu to Ishiki ni kansuru Chōsa Hōkoku Sho (Report on a Study of the Residential Life
and Attitudes of Residents of Tama New Town) (Tōkyō: Tōkyō-to Minami-tama Shintoshi
Kaihatsu Hombu, 1972).

4) were more likely to have seen the *danchi* as a terminal move before coming, and much more likely to want to stay once they were there.

5) are more likely to interact with their neighbors; and

6) participate more both in voluntary recreation and leisure-time clubs and groups, in *danchi*-organized activities such as cleanup efforts, and in *danchi* "self-government" associations.

No doubt education, income, and the ages of children have independent influences on community involvement; I maintain that perceptions of terminal mobility play a large role and cite in this regard the inclusion in the Tama study of a group of *home owners* in a subdivision in the New Town. These people have achieved the own-your-own-home ideal and, while socially and economically similar to the white-collar *danchi* residents, resemble the blue-collar people in their expectations of future physical mobility. In evaluation of their new residential area and participation in it, the home owners were significantly more like the blue-collar people with whom they shared very little except mobility expectations.

THE FUTURE OF THE POLITICAL COMMUNITY IN URBAN JAPAN

POSITIVE POTENTIAL

There are, in each of the communities covered in this study, persons who fall into the categories of those most likely to be involved in their neighborhoods in a variety of ways--primarily parents and partisans. Moreover, in those areas undergoing the most rapid social change, that is, the suburbs, the potential role of women in the community is increasing and the rising numbers of large, socially homogeneous *danchi* may signal an increase in the "organizable" proportion of the metropolitan population.

The participant proclivities of otherwise apathetic *danchi* residents may increase if, as noted by Christie Kiefer and Ralph Falconeri, physically immobilized population groups also grow. Their work along with this study suggest that expectations of future physical mobility have a negative influence on neighborhood involvement. As rising land prices push the goal of a single-family dwelling beyond the hopes of more and more *danchi*-dwellers and exit thus becomes a less realistic goal, overt loyalty to one's neighborhood and the voicing of dissatisfaction may become more frequently exercised.

Beyond the simple frequency in communities of persons most likely--demographically and ideologically--to be involved therein, one must direct attention to the nature of political issues in any effort to assess the potential for local-level political participation. Even in neighborhoods where "participant types" are rare, or where residential forms hinder action, there are often enough persons with the economic resources, educational skills, and even concrete experience to constitute a potential for significant action if the issue is right and the opportunities are there. This study and Margaret McKean's have uncovered many individuals now manifestly uninterested in community affairs who have in the past participated in a wide variety of neighborhood-based demand-making activities directed at the municipal authorities.

Moreover, there are in most neighborhoods organizations which can be--or at least are seen as--channels for demand-making: the *chōkai* or neighborhood associations. Margaret McKean has noted the frequent inability of such traditional organizations to make effective demands in the contemporary urban situation. Nevertheless, a number of studies have indicated rather clearly that the *chōkai* are still widely regarded by urbanites as interest articulation structures.[12] Indeed, this perception, rather than objective organizational capabilities, seems to be the crucial criterion for creating a potential for the initiation of action.

In addition to popular perceptions, the responsiveness and experience of the *chōkai* are relevant factors. *Chōkai* officials do see themselves as transmitters of local demands upward and profess willingness to intercede with the municipal authorities (Tokyo Shisei Chosa Kai, 1971:62-87). Moreover, *chōkai* do carry out a wide variety of (usually petty) demand-making activities concerning the needs of neighborhood residents and do in many instances establish the kind of ties with officials which at least invite action.

Given resources, skills, facilitating structures, and experience, all that is lacking are issues salient enough to induce action. If there are no such issues--that is, if political and environmental affairs do not cry out for remedy--then perhaps the citizens are entitled to some apoliticism. However, the influence of home ownership and parenthood suggests that immediate environmental problems, threats to children (physical

---

[12]Tokyō Shisei Chōsa Kai, pp. 122-27; Chōfu-shi, pp. 95-105; Isomura et al., p. 157; Matsumoto Tokuzo, "Shimin Ishiki no Kaihatsu to Jichitai" (The Development of Citizen Consciousness and the Municipality), Toshi Mondai, 62:7 (July 1971), p. 38.

or educational) or to home values, and incomplete or over-aged
urban facilities can stimulate immediate and powerful response.
The weak influence on active neighborhood involvement of many
of the demographic and socioeconomic variables analyzed above
may be due, as Margaret McKean suggests, to the overriding cata-
lytic influence of issues (see also Hariu Seikichi, 1971:10,14;
Iwai, 1971:139).

A final element hypothetically conducive to neighborhood
involvement by residents is geographical congruence--the degree
to which the neighborhood coincides physically with other politically meaningful entities such as school districts or election
precincts (Isomura *et al.*, p.139; Shinohara Hajime, personal communication, November 1971). The PTA is an arena for vociferous
parental participation in many areas: curricular matters, school
facilities, faculty performance, and a variety of transportation
and environmental problems related to pupil travel to and from
school.

In light of the central role of their children's education
in parental eyes, it would seem that the long-term goals of the
Tōkyō metropolitan government (which wants to nurture the residential neighborhood as a real community) would be well served
by the re-drawing of *machi* boundaries or school districts so
that they coincide. In this light also, the move by the Kanazawa
government to replace the *chōkai* (or *chōnaikai*, as they are
called there) with individual liaison representatives seems unwise, unless that city's administration does not share Tōkyō's
concern for neighborhood-level citizen involvement.

OBSTRUCTIONS TO COMMUNITY ACTION

The above, while indicating potential sources of community
involvement, should not give one the impression that the urban
Japanese neighborhood is peculiarly impervious to the "decline
of community" seen in large cities elsewhere in the industrial
world. The functions of the Japanese neighborhood in reducing
individual anomie and social disorganization during the period
of Japan's industrialization are peculiar, and may still be so;
nevertheless, as far as political involvement in the neighborhood
is concerned, Japanese society appears to be subject to the same
trends which are in motion in other advanced societies.[13]

First, the absolute numbers of those most likely to be
involved in their neighborhoods--early middle-aged, home-owning

---

[13]See, for instance, Robert Dahl, Who Governs? (New Haven: Yale University Press,
1961), chs. 24-26; Scott Greer, The Emerging City (New York: Free Press, 1962), pp. 105-06.

parents and political partisans--are few. In the present study,
only 6% of the entire sample were home-owning parents in their
40s and 50s (and even fewer were also long-time residents of
their *machi*), although larger numbers of respondents possessed
one or two of these characteristics. Partisanship was measured
on a nine-point scale; persons scoring on the three highest steps
of the scale constituted only 20% of the total sample, while
those on the top two totalled less than 10%.

In the analysis of these figures, however, two elements
must be considered. First, although one may, on the basis of
these figures, judge that the absolute potential for grassroots
democratic action in Japan is low, it may nevertheless match or
even surpass that in other democracies. Bradley Richardson
(1974: Chap.8) has presented data for the nation as a whole
which indicate that the popular roots of Japanese democracy,
although perhaps fragile, may in fact be as well dug in as they
are in most other industrial societies. Table 5 offers a frag-
mentary Japan-U.S. comparison: except in the case of campaigning
and organized neighborhood involvement, Tōkyō residents do not
appear significantly "inferior" to a national sample in America
(where residents of large cities do not participate strikingly
more than other people). Campaign participation in Japan is
hamstrung by a peculiarly restrictive set of laws; if this area
of participation is excluded, it is again clear that although
Japanese urban communities do not appear very activist, neither
do urban communities elsewhere.

Second, although participant individuals may be few in
any single urban neighborhood, they may nevertheless constitute
a critical mass sufficient to mobilize larger numbers of residents should the right issue arise. Although fewer than 10% of
the sample used in this study had ever contacted any political
official, participated politically in any way other than voting,
or participated in *chōkai* activities, between 20% and 30% were
active in neighboring, discussed political and local problems
with their neighbors, and/or had school-age children. Also,
roughly 50-60% felt satisfied with, owned a home in, and wanted
to stay in their neighborhood. Such persons, even if customarily
apathetic, are hardly deracinated or atomized, and the history
of citizens' movements shows that they can be mobilized.

The sorts of issues which effectively convert availability
into participation, however, are rather rare. The cases discussed by Margaret McKean and Ralph Falconeri are examples of
Japanese communities under stress, urban and rural. The "motley
procession to modernity" in most cases takes place *within* individuals, and apparently strikes communities as a whole only

TABLE 5

POLITICAL PARTICIPATION: JAPANESE AND AMERICANS
(% who say "yes" or perform act regularly)

Measures of Involvement	United States (national sample 1967)	Japan (national sample 1967)	Japan (7 largest cities 1967)	Tōkyō (1972)
Vote always or usually in national elections	71%	72%	64%	78%
Vote always or usually in local elections	47	--*	--	73
Attend political meetings or rallies	19	50	56	18
Member of political organization	8	4	4	3**
Participate in activities of neighborhood problem-solving organization	32	11	15[†]	9
Collaborate with neighbors in other manner to solve local problem	--	--	--	4
Contacted local official about a) social or local problem b) personal problem	14 / 7	11 / 7	18	13
Contacted extralocal official about a) social or local problem b) personal problem	11 / 6	5 / 3	8	14
Supported a candidate	28	--	--	6
Gave money in a campaign	13	--	--	1
Performed other campaign acts[††]	--	--(75)[§]	--(84)	1-6(84)

*No data.

**However, 42% were members of neighborhood associations, 10% of labor unions, and 1% of citizens' groups, all of which are frequently politically active.

[†]The data display from which this figure was taken is not clear as to whether the action was organizational or not, or both.

[††]In columns 2 and 3 the question referred to campaign participation in general; in column 4 the range covers responses to questions on 5 different forms of campaign participation.

[§]The figures in parentheses refer to the percentage of respondents who did not participate in any way.

SOURCES: Columns 1 and 2: Sidney Verba, Norman Nie, and Jae-on Kim, *The Modes of Democratic Participation* (Beverly Hills: Sage, 1971),p. 36. Reprinted with permission. Column 3: Ikeuchi Hajime (ed.), *Shimin Ishiki no Kenkyū* (Tōkyō: Tōkyō University Press, 1974),various tables (tables listed on pp. 551-65). Column 4: Author's data.

infrequently, or in a series of small steps spread over time so as to minimize the probability of collective response. When a community is struck all at once, the response is perhaps more likely to resemble that of Falconeri's Saiwai-cho rather than that of McKean's Shibushi or Takaido.

As suggested by the characteristics of participants and the nature of critical issues, most of the collective community-oriented participation which does occur is concerned with very localized problems--bus service to a new *danchi*, a dangerous intersection, or a single factory or new highway. Such simple problems can frequently be solved with a few calls or visits to City Hall; moreover, one common source of community political involvement--the inadequacy of urban services and facilities in new suburbs--fades over time. In both cases, the almost inevitable consequences is the evaporation of whatever activist organization might have been mobilized for the occasion, and a reduction in the general level of citizen involvement. The weakest characteristic of community action is that its goals are usually so narrow that when they are achieved, action ceases without any generalization to larger systematic issues, other organizations, or other localities with similar problems.

The Japanese are certainly not alone in this characteristic--neighborhood action seldom spills over into lasting organization or action in other countries either.[14] But, in any case, sustained mobilization and liaison by leaders or organizations outside the neighborhood seems necessary if such neighborhood activities are to outlive their initial goals; and the Japanese have on occasion expressly rejected such overarching organizations in the fear that it might factionalize or become the pawn of some political party (Ui Jun, personal communication, March 1975).

THE FUTURE OF THE COMMUNITY

This study suggests continued decline of the neighborhood as a significant political and social unit in the Japanese city, but not eclipse and certainly not the atomization of the urban population. The process of decline has been documented and explained in the United States by Roland Warren (1972) and Sidney Verba and Norman Nie (1972), and observed in Japan by all three

---

[14]Wayne Cornelius and Henry Dietz, "Urbanization, Demand-making, and Political System Overload," paper presented at the annual meeting of the American Political Science Association, 1973, pp. 31-37; Irving Horowitz, ed. Masses in Latin America (New York: Oxford University Press, 1970), esp. chs. by Bryan Roberts, Daniel Goldrich et al., and Julio Cotler.

of the papers included here. But, as many have pointed out, disintegration and anomie are not the result. The nuclear family and
nonlocal kin, friends, formal organizations, and work groups involve the vast majority of individuals in a satisfying, gratifying
network which simultaneously protects the individual desire for
privacy and the Japanese desire for warm, *gemeinschaftlich* groups.
In Japan the maintenance of individual psychic and social security
amid the flux and complexity of the city has been documented by
many writers who have, one should note, all credited the urban
neighborhood with a significant, although not necessarily primary, role in the maintenance of social order and control and
the distribution of both tangible and intangible forms of support.[15] The local neighborhood may not be a true community, but
it protects (except perhaps in the *danchi*) the liberty, equality,
and privacy which so many migrants to the city find so gratifying.

In addition to these *shimboku* (intimacy, friendship) functions performed by the urban neighborhood and its organizations,
administrative functions--liaison or *renraku* and cooperation or
kyōryoku--served by the neighborhood will continue to round out
the "three *ku*" of neighborhood functions which will prevent the
eclipse of the Japanese urban neighborhood.[16] *Renraku* frequently
includes the articulation upward of residents' desires, but is
predominantly a downward communication flow, the dissemination
of information about government programs and goals right down to
the individual household by volunteer neighborhood association
members, at no cost to the taxpayers. *Kyōryoku* includes more
active forms of administrative activities: neighborhood associations collect statistics, distribute pesticides, clean streets,
keep crime and fire prevention watches, maintain roads and parks,
repair streetlights, maintain sewers, and perform many other
functions seen elsewhere as governmental. The load of delegated
functions is heavy--in one survey in Tōkyō, three-quarters of a
sample of *chōkai* officials said that they performed duties which
they wished the government would handle and that governmental
requests were excessive.[17]

By bearing the workload imposed from above, the neighborhood associations are probably giving the Japanese better government at far less cost than would otherwise be possible, but one
wonders if local autonomy and initiative can survive the

---

[15]See, inter alia, Suzuki Eitarō (1957); Yazaki Takeo (1963:46, 255–68); R.P. Dore
(1967:138ff, 255); and Ezra Vogel (1963).

[16]Unless, of course, such potentially counterproductive efforts to bypass the machi
as the Kanazawa administrative liaison system become widespread.

[17]Tōkyō Shisei Chōsa Kai, pp. 56–60.

co-optation and workload. Still, as long as the government is
"on its side," the urban neighborhood will survive as a political
entity, and thus survive as a unit of potential political mobilization. And it will no doubt continue to wrest concessions and
benefits from the government on a small scale, but this tactical
success may, as Margaret McKean suggests, be combined with a
well-founded strategic pessimism among the urban populace.

Such movements as those studied by Professor McKean, and
many less coherent and vigorous ones, seem consistently (and
sometimes easily) successful at working within the system, but
their participants remain cynical and distrustful and are, indeed, busy and justly concerned with a host of nonpolitical concerns such as job and family. The systemic implications of
their actions and the arenas in which the national manifestations
of their problems can be solved are too distant; involvement requires too much time and effort; local leaders are often inept;
and on a grander scale the issues are tied up with corporate
and political interests largely impervious to any but the most
massive public outcry. The Japanese, like urbanites around
the world, are finding that their problems are growing beyond
the neighborhood to the level of City Hall and Parliament; concern
for the neighborhood correspondingly declines, as does overall
political activism as the realization sinks in that more distant
branches of government are less responsive. Japanese urbanites
remain very sensitive to certain stimuli, and possessed of the
resources to make themselves heard and effective locally, like
a sort of urban minutmen. But while minutemen may win many a
skirmish, they do not win wars.

APPENDIX A

THE STUDY SAMPLE

After discussion with Japanese sociologists and reference
to a variety of Japanese sources, some of which are cited in Note
3, it was decided that the most parsimonious, yet meaningful,
categorization of areas within metropolitan Tōkyō was: central
city or downtown (*shitamachi*), urban residential or uptown (*yamanote*), and suburbs. To test this assumption, data were collected
for all the cities and wards of Tōkyō from the *Tōkyō Tōkei Nenkan*
(*Tōkyō Statistical Yearbook [1969]*) on a variety of social and
economic indicators. A clear *shitamachi-yamanote* continuum
emerged among the wards, with *shitamachi* wards relatively: low
in per capita income; low in gross population turnover but high
in net out-migration; low in floor space per capita; and high in
frequency of industrial enterprises, especially small-scale enterprises. *Yamanote* wards clustered at the other ends of these measures. The two polar cases--Sumida ward in the *shitamachi* and
Shibuya ward in the *yamanote*--were selected and within each a
single *machi* or neighborhood (the smallest urban administrative
unit in Japan) was chosen for intensive study. The *machi* were
chosen in a manner similar to the wards, using the same data:
a small number of *machi* roughly representative of the entire
ward on the indices used previously were located, and their number was reduced by eliminating those too large (over 1,000 families) for easy participant observation by a single person. The
remaining *machi*--about five in each ward--were visited; a few were
ruled out by exceptional conditions: the presence of a factory
or *danchi* which dominated the entire neighborhood, or the pre-
dominance of a single social class. One was chosen from the final
two or three by an admittedly intuitive estimate of its relative
representativeness of the entire ward.

The suburban cities surrounding Tōkyō were also measured
on the social and economic indices discussed above, but did not
fit clearly on the continuum. The defining characteristics of
the suburbs appeared to be rapid population growth, high net
in-migration, high frequency of out-commutation, and low levels
of industrialization. A rather typical--but not extremely fast-
growing--city was selected, Chōfu; and a *machi* was chosen from
within that city by a process similar to that used in neighborhood selection in the ward area.

About eight months of frequent visits to and numerous con-
versations in each *machi* followed, culminating in May 1972 with
the data presented here. The sample was chosen randomly from the
lists of residents in each of the three *machi* on record in their
respective city halls or ward offices.

REFERENCES

Chōfu-shi, Sōmu-bu, Kikaku-shitsu. *Chōfu Shimin no Ishiki Chōsa Sho* (Report on a Survey of Citizens' Attitudes in Chōfu). Tokyō: Chōfu-shi, Sōmu-bu, Kikaku-shitsu, 1971.

Cornelius, Wayne, and Henry Dietz. "Urbanization, Demand-making, and Political System Overload." Paper presented at the annual meeting of the American Political Science Association, New Orleans, 1973.

Dahl, Robert. *Who Governs?* New Haven: Yale University Press, 1961.

Dore, Ronald P. *City Life in Japan.* Berkeley: University of California Press, 1967.

Greer, Scott. *The Emerging City.* New York: Free Press, 1962.

Hariu Seikichi. "Jūmin Ishiki no Kihonteki Sai-Kentō" (A Fundamental Reappraisal of Citizen Consciousness). *Toshi Mondai*, 62:7 (July 1963), 10, 14.

Hayashi Chikio et al., eds. *Dai Ni Nihonjin no Kokuminsei* (The Japanese National Character: Book Two). Tokyō: Shiseidō, 1970), see especially pages 557, Q. 4.4, 560, Q. 5.6.

Horowitz, Irving, ed. *Masses in Latin America.* New York: Oxford University Press, 1970.

Ikeuchi Hajime, ed. *Shimin Ishiki no Kenkyū* (A Study of Citizen Consciousness). Tokyō: Tokyō University Press, 1974.

Isomura Eiichi et al. *Toshi Keisei no Ronri to Jūmin* (Urban Residents and The Logic of City Formation). Tokyō: Tokyō University Press, 1971.

Iwai Hiroaki, ed. *Toshi Shakaigaku* (Urban Sociology). Tokyō: Yuhikaku, 1971.

Kokumin Seikatsu Shingikai, ed. *Komyunitei* (Community). Tokyō: Okura-shō, 1970.

Kurasawa Susumu. "Danchi Jūmin to Jimoto Jūmin (Danchi Residents and Local Residents). *Toshi Mondai*, 58:12 (December 1967), 55ff.

_____. *Nihon no Toshi Shakai* (Japanese Urban Society). Tokyō: Fukumura, 1968.

Kuroda, Toshio, "Trends in Internal Migration and Policy Questions in Japan." *Paper presented at the International Population Conference, Liege, Belgium, 1973.*

Matsumoto Tokuzō. "Shimin Ishiki no Kaihatsu to Jichitai" (The Development of Citizen Consciousness and the Municipality). *Toshi Mondai*, 62:7 (July 1971), 38.

Nakamura Hachirō. "Toshi ni okeru Jūmin Ruikei" (A Typology of Urban Residents), *Toshi Mondai*, 58:6 (June 1967), 61-66.

Nakane, Chie. *Japanese Society.* Berkeley: University of California Press, 1970.

Richardson, Bradley. *The Political Culture of Japan.* Berkeley: University of California Press, 1974:Ch. 8.

Sumida-ku, Kōho-shitsu. *Sumida Kusei Yoron Chōsa* (A Study of Public Opinions Regarding the Sumida Ward Government). *Tōkyō: Sumida-ku, Kōho-shitsu, 1971.*

Suzuki Eitarō. *Toshi Shakaigaku Genri* (Principles of Urban Sociology). *Tōkyō: Yuhikaku, 1957.*

Suzuki Hiroshi et al., *Toshi Shakai ni okeru Seiji Ishiki to Riidashippu* (Political Attitudes and Leadership in Urban Society). *Fukuoka: Fukuoka-ken Senkyu Kenri Iinkai, 1968.*

Tōkyō Shisei Chōsa Kai. *Tōkyō ni okeru Chiiki Shakai Shoshiki* (Local Organization in Tōkyō). *Tōkyō: Tōkyō Shisei Chōsa Kai, 1971.*

Tōkyō Tōkei Kyōkai. *Tokyo Statistical Yearbook, 1969.* *Tōkyō: Tōkyō Tōkei Kyōkai, 1969.*

Tōkyō-to Minami-tama Shintoshi Kaihatsu Hombu. *Tama Nyū Taun Kyojūsha no Jū-seikatsu to Ishiki ni kansuru Chōsa Hōkoku Sho* (Report on a Study of the Residential Life and Attitudes of Residents of Tama New Town). *Tōkyō: Tōkyō-to Minami-tama Shintoshi Kaihatsu Hombu, 1972.*

Tōkyō-to, Sōmu-kyoku, Tōkei-bu. *Jinkō no Ugoki* (Population Movement). *Tokyo: Tōkyō-to, Sōmu-kyoku, Tōkei-bu, annual.*

Tsushima Sadao et al. "Toshi Shūdan Jūtakuchi ni okeru Kinrin Kankei" (Neighboring Relationships in an Urban Mass Housing Project), *Shakaigaku Kenkyū*, No. 19 (November 1960), 20-21.

Ui Jun. *Personal communication,* March 1975.

Verba, Sidney, and Norman Nie. *Participation in America.* New
York: Harper and Row, 1972.

Vogel, Ezra. *Japan's New Middle Class.* Berkeley: University of
California Press, 1963.

Warren, Roland. *The Community in America.* Chicago: Rand McNally,
1972.

Watanuki, Jōji. "Change and Persistence in Socio-Political Behavior: Japanese Case." *Unpublished paper, Sophia University, Tokyo, 1972.*

_____. "Patterns of Politics in Present-day Japan." *Party
Systems and Voter Alignments.* Edited by Seymour Lipset
and Stein Rokkan. New York: Free Press, 1967.

White, James. "Political Aspects of Internal Migration." *Internal Migration in Industrial Societies.* Edited by
George Myers. Durham: Duke University Press, forthcoming.

_____. "Social Status and Political Participation in Tokyo."
*Unpublished paper, University of North Carolina, Chapel
Hill, 1975.*

Yamamoto Noboru. "Shinjū Shimin no Jichi Ishiki" (Attitudes Regarding Political Autonomy Among New Urbanites). *Toshi
Mondai* 56:5 (May 1965).

Yazaki Takeo. *The Japanese City.* Translated by David Swain.
Rutland: Japan Publications Trading Co., 1963.

beddo taun ベッドタウン

    bed town

chō 町

    a street; a block; often
    a town

chōkai 町会

    see *chōnaikai*

chōkaichō 町会長

    neighborhood association
    chief

chōnaikai 町内会

    neighborhood association

chōnaikaichō 町内会長

    see *chōkaichō*

danchi 団地

    high rise apartment build-
    ing complex; usu. high rise

danchi zoku 団地族

    danchi residents

Edo 江戸

    feudal-period name for
    present *Tōkyō*

fujinbu 婦人部

    women's auxiliary

gemeinschaft ゲマインシャフト

    a spontaneously arising
    social relationship charac-
    terized by strong reciprocal
    bonds of sentiment and/or
    kinship within a common
    code of tradition

geshukunin papa 下宿人パパ

    lodger papa

gesellschaft ゲゼルシャフト

    a rationally developed,
    mechanistic-type of so-
    cial relationship charac-
    terized by impersonal as-
    sociations between persons

gyōsei renrakuin seido 行政連絡員制度

    administrative liaison
    system

hanchō 班長

    leader of a *chōnaikai* areal
    subdivision

ie 家

    extended patrilineal
    family

ikuji noirōze 育児ノイローゼ

    child-rearing neurosis

jūmin undō 住民運動

    residents' movement; a
    social movement protesting
    a problem in a particular
    locality, composed of
    people who all reside in
    that area

kairanban 回覧板

    circulating notice board

kindaiteki 近代的

    modernistic

kodomokai 子供会

    children's group

kodomo wa komyunitei no kasugai
子供はコミュニティの鎹

    "the community whose
    children play together
    stays together"; lit.,
    children are the adhesive
    of the community

kombinat コンビナート
> industrial combine; a Russian word, pronounced "kombinato" in Japanese, refering to massive complexes of factories in related industries

kyōroku 協力
> cooperation

machi 町
> see chō

mai-hōmu-shugi マイホーム主義
> my-home-ism

mukō no hitotachi 向うの人達
> "those people over there"; or "people on the other side"

mukō sangen ryō tonari 向う三軒両隣
> two houses, one on either side, and the three houses directly across the street

okami 御上
> superior; used today primarily to refer to local authorities

rejā būmu レジャー ブーム
> leisure boom

renraku 連絡
> liaison

renrakuin 連絡員
> liaison system

rinpō han 隣邦班
> neighborhood areal subdivision of a chōnaikai; usually from 10-25 families

sake 酒
> Japanese rice wine

samurai 侍
> Japanese feudal warrior

sarariiman サラリー マン
> salaryman; white-collar worker

seinenbu 青年部
> usually young man or men, or youth (in this study refers to both young men and women) division

shataku 社宅
> company-owned danchi

shikata ga nai 仕方がない
> "it can't be helped"; or "it's inevitable"

shimboku 親睦
> intimacy; friendship

shimpoteki 進歩的
> progressive

shitamachi 下町
> central city; downtown

shōtenkai 商店会
> businessmen's association; shopkeepers' association

sōkaiya 総会屋
> those who maintain order (silent dissent) at shareholders' meetings.

tatami 畳
> straw mats used for floor coverings in Japanese homes

tofū 豆腐
> bean curd

Tōkaidō 東海道
> eastern seacoast highway

ūman ribbu ウーマン リブ
> women's liberation

yamanote 山の手
> urban residental district;
> uptown

yen 円

> Japanese currency, 1976
> valuation is approximately
> ¥ 300 per US $1.00

yūryokusha 有力者
> those who hold power; usually
> local notables or political
> bosses and generally linked
> to the conservative LDP; not
> necessarily pejorative in
> connoation